HAUNTED
WORTHING

HAUNTED WORTHING

Wendy Hughes

First published 2010

The History Press
The Mill, Brimscombe Port
Stroud, Gloucestershire, GL5 2QG
www.thehistorypress.co.uk

British Library Cataloguing in Publication Data.
A catalogue record for this book is available from the British Library.

ISBN 978 0 7524 5616 4

Typesetting and origination by The History Press
Printed in Great Britain
Manufacturing managed by Jellyfish Print Solutions Ltd

Contents

About the Author

Wendy Hughes was born and brought up a stone's throw from the Gower Peninsula in Swansea, South Wales. She has been writing since 1989, and has always been enthralled by the tales of everyday people, ghosts, folklore, eccentricities and the quirky side of life. Wendy has written numerous books and articles on local history, especially concerning the traditions and customs of her native Wales. She thoroughly enjoys exploring a new topic or researching a different viewpoint on a subject. She now lives close to the sea at Rustington in West Sussex with her husband Conrad, and they have two grown-up sons.

Acknowledgements

I would like to express my thanks to all the writers who have written on the subject of the supernatural before me and without whom I could not have started the research for this book. A select bibliography is included at the end of this book. Special thanks, in no particular order, must go to:

Andrew House of Supernatural Tours (www.supernatural-tours.co.uk) for his comprehensive information on ghosts.

Arron Weedall, who has written *Haunted Chichester and Beyond* and runs the WSPI website (www.wspi.co.uk), and Stuart Logan of Children of the City Paranormal Investigations (www.cotcpi.co.uk), for their help with local stories, especially concerning Sompting Church and Clapham Wood.

Neil Rogers-Davis for his help with the stories concerning Angmering, and for his excellent website (www.angmeringvillage.co.uk).

Mr Peter Thorogood and Mr Roger Linton for a fascinating insight into the history of St Mary's at Bramber and their foresight ensuring that St Mary's was saved for future generations to enjoy.

Ivor and Yvonne Holland of Quality Textiles, Littlehampton, for telling me so much about their building and allowing me to take photographs.

Ellie Boiling and Katie Smith of the Dolphin Hotel, Littlehampton, for introducing me to their 'family' of spirits and for the experience. Also thank you for allowing me to take photographs.

Rosie Gray, Theatres Administration Officer, Worthing Theatres, for information concerning the Grey Lady and the Connaught Theatre.

Jacqueline Simpson for allowing me to use one of the photographs included in her book *Folklore of Sussex*, and also for snippets of information.

Martin Hayes and the staff of West Sussex County Council Library Service for their constant help and friendly service.

West Sussex Past Pictures website (www.westsussexpast.org.uk), which has over 11,500 images of the area and allowed me to use several archive photographs in this book.

Janet Cameron for her help with Shoreham and also for allowing me to use some of the photographs used in her book, entitled *Paranormal Brighton and Hove*.

Joyce Elsden, Jean Robertson and Peggy Green for sharing their paranormal experience at Sompting with me.

Last, but certainly not least, Conrad Hughes for his skilful editing of the final draft and saving me from publishing too many silly mistakes. Also for giving up so much of his valuable time driving me to interviews and taking the majority of the photographs for this book, in all weathers!

Introduction

As a relative newcomer to the Worthing area, which I have now made my home, I am delighted to discover that it has a rich and enthralling history, much of which still needs to be explored fully. In my study of ghostly encounters in and around the Worthing area, I have noticed that, on the whole, there are no horrific tales of ghosts jumping out, no thundering crashes or frightening unseen forces throwing objects at uninvited guests. The majority of ghosts that choose to frequent the area are friendlier and more peaceful than those encountered in other places, with the exception of one or two who have a sad past.

So what exactly is a ghost? Every culture in the world has its stories concerning ghosts and often there are conflicting beliefs as to what ghosts really are or indeed, as some will say, if they exist at all. Are they just a figment of one's imagination or are they part of reality? A ghost is thought to be a manifestation of the spirit or soul of a person who, for some reason, has remained on earth after his or her death. I spoke to several ghost researchers when writing this book and most approach the subject from a more scientific point of view, seeking to establish a relationship between recorded phenomena and the presence of a ghost. Some told me that ghosts are not actual souls or spirits, but are the psychic energy left behind by the deceased which is experienced by people who are sensitive to its presence.

However, if this is the case, this does not explain those ghosts that answer questions or carry out actions requested by living people. Sometimes ghosts are associated with disturbances thought to be due to electromagnetic fields, and paranormal investigators using field detectors today are finding 'ghostly' results near wall outlets and electrical appliances. It would appear that most investigators share some basic beliefs about ghosts, such as spirits frequent places they visited when they were alive or where they died, and apparitions often wear clothing they would have worn when they lived. Some of the most popular places which are haunted are burial grounds, cemeteries, sacred ancient sites, places where violence occurred, theatres, ancient ruins, castles and, of course, homes. This is certainly true of the hauntings I have found in and around Worthing.

Ghosts make contact with us through various senses such as sight, smell, touch and hearing. For example, a ghost may attract our attention by flicking lights on and off or moving objects. These ghosts are called poltergeists or noisy ghosts, and are merely using their energy to attract attention. Certainly this is the case at the Dolphin Hotel in Littlehampton. We may see a spirit or a shadow on the edge of our field of vision. Fragrances associated with a spirit in life are also very common, such as incense in the case of monks (St Mary's at Bramber is a perfect example of this), a favourite perfume or the smell of a cigar when a spirit has smoked in their previous life. Other ghosts make their presence known through touch or a kiss, a chill on the back of the neck, a cold breeze passing through a room, or the feeling of someone sitting or lying in a bed. Other spirits prefer to communicate through taps, bumps or footsteps walking across a room. Interestingly, most of the stories in this book can be placed in one or more of these categories.

So why do ghosts haunt people or places? It would appear that often the spirit wishes to convey a message before moving to a higher realm, for example when someone has been murdered, committed suicide or something relating to their or another person's death. The ghost may have some unfinished business, such as finding lost papers, a will or hidden treasure. In some circumstances, particularly if the death was instantaneous, the ghost may not realise they are dead, or they chose to remain part of a family or the home where they once lived. Sometimes when the death of souls has been tragic their appearance may be triggered by the anniversary of the death. As with everything, there are some ghosts that are positive and others that give off negative energy. An apparition can be seen by one or more people at the same time, but there are also instances where only one person in a room can see the ghost whilst others see nothing. Again, most of the stories in this book fall into one of these categories.

I can only assume that the ghostly spirits encountered in and around Worthing are content to haunt for their own special reasons and blend into their environment, 'living' in harmony with present-day human beings. Where possible, I have tried to add a balanced mixture of historical fact to place the haunting in its context, and I hope the reader will sit back and enjoy this book, judge for themselves the nature of the supernatural and be inspired to find out and learn a little more about historic Worthing.

Wendy Hughes,
2010

1

Around the Town

Worthing is not just a seaside resort made famous in 1798 when Princess Amelia, youngest daughter of George III, arrived to convalesce from a lame knee, but it has a history that dates back to prehistoric times.

The town grew from a tiny, coastal, mackerel-fishing hamlet recorded as 'Ordinge' in 1086 with a population of just twenty-two. In the thirteenth century it became known as 'Worth' or 'Wurtha ingas', which means 'the settlement belonging to the people of Worth or Wurth'. It predominately remained an agricultural and fishing hamlet for centuries until the arrival, in the 1750s, of wealthy visitors whose needs, such as lodging houses, a theatre, libraries and bathing establishments, were met. In 1803 Worthing became a town, and from 1810 a market provided supplies of fresh fish, poultry and vegetables, 'always in abundance and of the first quality'. A guidebook of 1814 describes the shops as being 'filled with articles well assorted for a family'. The area became a stronghold for smugglers in the nineteenth century, and Oscar Wilde holidayed in the town in 1893 and again in 1894 when he wrote *The Importance of Being Earnest*. The town received its Royal Charter in 1890 and the Borough crest was created with the inscription '*Ex Terra Compiam E Mari Salutem*', meaning 'From the Land Wealth and the Sea Health'.

The town become the home to several literary figures, including the Nobel Prize winner Harold Pinter. Worthing was also home to several military divisions in preparation for the D-Day landings. Once Worthing had many historic buildings of unique quality, but like many places during the 1960s and '70s some of the oldest buildings were demolished to make way for what many consider Worthing's biggest planning disaster, the Guildbourne Centre. Historic places like the Theatre Royal in Ann Street and the Royal George, the town's oldest public house, both well-known landmarks of the town, were lost forever.

Lady in Grey

Ask any actor who began their career by performing at Worthing and most will tell you that working at the Connaught Theatre in Union Place ensured a prosperous career. Actors also claim that to see a theatre ghost brings good luck and guarantees success for the play being staged at that time. Few claim to have actually seen the Grey Lady reputed to haunt the Connaught Theatre, but perhaps she does bring good luck to this delightful theatre which celebrates its seventy-fifth anniversary in 2010.

The Connaught Theatre building started life on 29 January 1914 as the Picturedrome, the first purpose-built cinema in Worthing, and was situated at the south side of Union Place, a few yards from the corner of Chapel Road. As the popularity of Worthing grew and the demand for entertainment increased, the Connaught Hall was built in

1916 adjacent to the Picturedrome and amateur dramas and dances were staged there. A resident company performed plays weekly, but their existence was put in jeopardy by the opening of the Pier Pavilion in 1926. By 1929 the New Theatre Royal in Bath Place, which was then the centre of productions in Worthing, was threatened with closure. Stage manager and theatre impresario Walter Lindsay, who had developed repertory in the town, was furious that the New Theatre Royal was being threatened and found an alternative venue at the Connaught Hall. He converted it into a theatre and, despite mounting debts, continued to maintain drama in Worthing, but soon it failed. However, in 1932 Charles William Bell and William Simon Fraser presented their first season of repertory productions at the Connaught Hall, having seen the success in Brighton and the West End in London. The company went from strength to strength and changed its name from the Mask Players to the ill-fated Worthing Repertory Co. In 1935 Carl Adolph Seebold took over and converted the Picturedrome into the much larger New Connaught Theatre, with the Connaught Hall subsequently being known as the Old Connaught Theatre, the Home Guard Garrison Theatre and the Ritz Ballroom before finally becoming the Ritz, as it is known today.

Bell and Fraser played their final performance of *Happy Ending* at the Connaught Hall on 28 September 1935, just forty-eight hours before the opening of the newly refurbished art deco New Connaught Theatre. The opening night was a resounding success, with between 5,000 and 6,000 requests for tickets for just 920 seats. Bell and Fraser were toasted in the bar of the New Connaught Theatre, which was the largest theatrical bar in the country at the time. The theatre continued under private management for the next thirty years, but eventually closed as a commercial venture in 1966 when it was purchased by the local council and reopened in 1967 under trustee management. Since 1999 the Connaught has been under the management of Worthing Borough Council. Illustrious names to have trodden the boards at Worthing include Patricia Routledge, Christopher Lee, Peter Cushing, Ian Holm, Susannah York, June Whitfield and David Suchet, whilst writers such as Alan Ayckbourn, Harold Pinter and Ray Cooney have all learnt their craft at the theatre where their work continues to be performed.

None of the present staff at the Connaught Theatre have actually seen the Grey Lady, although one thought she saw a fleeting glimpse of a figure passing by the rear of the auditorium, but when she looked again all she saw was the curtain flapping as though someone had passed by. The Grey Lady, it seems, particularly likes Box 4, from where she can oversee a performance. The apparition of this actress wears a grey dress, though unusually its style has been placed in several periods, maybe depending on the different roles she played in life. Some say she wears a grey shawl and has a slim, pale face with dark pool-like eyes, but all agree she is friendly.

It seems she has been a resident of the Connaught for quite a while. An electrician who worked at the theatre for over twenty years never saw the ghost himself, but recalls stories that have been told to him. In 1974, after a matinée performance, one of the actors was walking along a corridor behind the scenes and happened to glance into the old No. 1 dressing room and was puzzled to see the figure of a fairly young woman in a long, grey gown sitting in front of the mirror applying her make-up. He continued to the end of the passage before suddenly realising that it was an odd time for the lady to be putting

The Connaught Theatre, showing the art deco façade, c. 1935.

The Connaught Theatre, 2010. Who is the Grey Lady that resides here?

make-up on as the performance had ended and everyone had left the building. He turned and retraced his steps and found the dressing room empty.

In 1987 Joseph Hall, who was a trainee at the theatre, went to fetch an item from beneath the stage, and on returning via the spiral staircase realised that he has come face to face with the Grey Lady on the stairs. Joseph explained, 'She was wearing a sort of Victorian dress, but I am afraid I didn't stay long enough to study her in more detail'. Others agree that there is something at the bottom of the stairway that causes people to shiver, especially at night.

A few years ago some workmen were called in to lay carpet in the foyer of the Connaught Theatre. As it happened, one was a Druid and the other a spiritualist, but they both saw the form of a lady dressed in grey with a 1930s hairdo. This does not appear to fit in with other sightings where she seems to be from a much earlier period. The manager took one of the carpet layers into the theatre administrator's office because he knew she was interested in such things. The worker then went into one of the boxes where he felt the Grey Lady had gone and tried to talk to her, but she drew further away from him and would not communicate.

To celebrate its seventy-fifth anniversary, the Connaught's main auditorium has been refurbished with new seating and carpeting, although the carpet is laid over the original parquet flooring. Whether you believe in the existence of the Grey Lady or not, the Connaught has been lucky enough to survive for seventy-five years and is set to survive well into the twenty-first century.

A Ghostly Image from the Past or a Victim of Crime?

Not far from the Connaught Theatre is Haverfield House, which became the headquarters of the Worthing Conservative Association on 1 July 1954. Prior to the house being built the land was a meadow. A road was constructed and more houses quickly followed. No. 4, which is now Haverfield House, was the last to be built and Nos 1, 2 and 3 have since been demolished to make way for the Post Office, West Sussex College of Arts and the Adult Education Centre. From the time it was built until around 1925, No. 4 Union Place was a private house, and for a short time it appears to have been known as Dawlish Lodge. From 1925 until 1944 it become a girls' school run by Miss Dutton and Miss Elliot before passing into the hands of the British Legion. It would appear the name Haverfield came into existence about the time the house became a school.

A strange incident began to unfold when it was reported in the *Worthing Herald* on 26 November 1954 that a suspected unexploded German bomb had been found in the grounds of Haverfield House. At the time the building housed the staff of the Worthing Conservative Association, who kept a close eye on the hole which appeared in the lawn at the rear of the house. The then caretaker, Harry Miller, thrust an 8ft pole into the hole but could not reach the bottom and realised it was obviously very deep. A search through the old maps of the town by the Town Hall officials revealed no sign of a well, and when the police arrived their only comment was, 'We do not think it is dangerous'. Various officials visited but, after surveying the hole, were left puzzled. The Conservative agent Mr Peter Livingstone thought that an underground stream might have been responsible for the hole, whilst others suggested that it may have been a natural subsidence, an old cesspool, a covered fishpond or even an ancient priests' tunnel. Eventually there was to be another far more interesting theory about the hole, which by now had developed from a small dip in the lawn into a large crater, causing it to be roped off for safety. A Royal Engineers bomb-disposal squad was called in and spent most of the week shifting many tons of earth. After the Royal Engineers had probed a distance of some 15ft, they found a cavity, sloping at the correct angle and about the right size for a 500lb bomb. A square of turf about 12ft across was raised and excavation carried out. Owing to the sandy subsoil, timber had to be used to shore up the sides until experts were satisfied that that no bomb lurked below the surface, and they could dismiss the theory of the unexploded German bomb. However, it was the *Worthing Herald* issue of 10 December 1954 that announced that Haverfield House did not have a bomb, but a ghost!

At this point, a more sinister explanation came to light. Although the old records relating to the property showed there were no wells, they revealed that once there might have been a tunnel leading to an old wine cellar under Haverfield House, or perhaps a sewer or drain.

Mrs A. Tribe of Oxford Road, who had lived in Haverfield House with her engineer husband until the end of the First World War, assured investigators that the grounds had not been dug other than to construct a children's sandpit, although she could remember a duck pond, which has since disappeared. However, it was Mrs Tribe's granddaughter, a Mrs H. Rea of Hamilton, Ontario, in Canada, who first revealed the story of the Haverfield House ghost. Mrs Rea had married a Canadian soldier and emigrated to Canada with her mother some eight years earlier, and said the house had a ghost of a beautiful young woman whom she claimed her mother actually had seen. It would appear that the ghost was often seen about the house and the sound of her footsteps could be heard clearly on the stairs. She understood that the people who bought the place from her grandparents could not keep their servants because of it.

When asked to describe the ghost, Mrs Rea said, 'My mother was in her bedroom one night when she heard footsteps and also thought she heard her sister calling her. She went out onto the landing and came face to face with a young woman wearing a dressing gown'. On hearing the story everyone wondered if there could be a connection between the ghost and the mystery hole. At the time there was a strong suspicion that there might be and the sergeant in charge of the excavation squad certainly believed so. As the men bored deeper they went straight through what resembled a layer of soft concrete and came across a large cavity which suggested a cellar under an older building. Was the girl a ghostly image from a grisly past, perhaps the victim of some crime perpetrated in the earlier house? Or for some reason did she lock herself away, perhaps after a forbidden romance, and die of a broken heart? Maybe there is some innocent explanation for her ghostly wanderings, but without further evidence we can only surmise.

Haverfield House. Who is the beautiful young woman seen on the stairs?

Murdered in a Brawl

On 2 May 1969 the *Worthing Herald* carried a report about the Dragoon public house in Market Street, where the Guildbourne Shopping Centre stands today, which was reputed to have a ghost and was due to be demolished on 17 May under the central area redevelopment scheme, probably to be replaced by a new pub. The pub was originally opened in 1820 and was formally known as the Volunteer. Before that it was a doss-house. More recently the Dragoon became known as the local home of modern jazz and was a popular meeting place for people from the theatrical world. The then licensee, Neil Murrich, and his wife Betty, had been there for two and a half years, and were going to take over a new pub in Ipswich. Neil, together with his brother-in-law Teddy Broughton, had built up the Dragoon within the jazz world. Teddy formerly played bass with the Malcolm Mitchell Trio bass player, and now played at the Dragoon with the John Greenwood Quartet, a group that always had a loyal following amongst local modern jazz enthusiasts. Apparently, many years ago, when the Dragoon was a rough house, a man met his death in a fight on the pavement outside and some say it is his spirit that used to haunt the pub. The spirit, who is tall and dressed in white, was reported as making an appearance every night between 6 p.m. and 7 p.m. Is there is significance to the timing I wonder? Was the ghost looking for his killer before the public house was finally closed forever? More importantly, what happened to him after the Dragoon was demolished?

Another ghostly tale is told of a private house that once stood on the nearby High Street, which extended past the present High Street along the ancient path from Broadwater. At one time the house was used by smugglers as an escape route via a tunnel leading from the site of the Old Worthing police station cells to a nearby pub, although we are not informed which one! Could this have been the Dragoon in the days of smuggling? Heavy but ghostly footsteps were heard repeatedly bounding up the stairway in the evenings. Could this be the ghost of a smuggler trying to hide his hoard, or is it the ghostly sounds of someone who was locked in the cells and died trying to escape? As this is one of the oldest parts of Worthing, it is little wonder that there is so much paranormal activity and a favourite haunt amongst ghosts.

Within the same vicinity there appears to be a ghost in the basement bookstore of Worthing Library. The gentleman is harmless and shuffles around wearing a long coat. Some of the staff have seen him, but as he appears to be friendly no one seems too concerned.

Who Are the Children Who Look Out on Montague Street?

Above Thornton's and Ernest Jones in Montague Street, in the centre of Worthing, the figures of two children have been caught on security cameras looking out of the windows of both shops. Over the years, members of staff have reported strange sounds coming from the upstairs rooms as well as things being moved around, even though they know no one is there. One staff member observed a ghostly figure in one of the storerooms and when asked what they were doing, the apparition spoke the word 'quiet'. Who are these children, one wonders, and why do they continue to haunt the premises?

Walking Monks

An interesting report of a haunted house appeared in the form of a letter sent in by an *Advertiser* reader, Walter Brazier, and was reprinted in the 'From Our Files' series in the *Worthing and District Advertiser* on 28 October 1987. It seems that in 1931 a couple with a young family moved into a house in Cobden Road, Worthing. Within a week they were back at the solicitors' office in an extremely distressed state, refusing to stay in the property for a moment longer, claiming that it was haunted. They said they had heard heavy footsteps rushing up and down the stairs and doors slamming shut. Hooded figures of monks were seen walking about 6in above the level of the present floors. Eventually, the landlord agreed that the tenancy should be terminated and admitted that it was not the first time that tenants had refused to stay in the house. Walter Brazier, who worked for the solicitors at the time, said he remembered the case well as it was the only authentic case of haunting that he had come across in his entire career. The house, as far as Mr Brazier could recall, was one of those on the south side of the road facing the Cobden Arms public house. The firm of solicitors held a copy of the manorial rolls for 1400 and they could not find any evidence of a former monastery on the site, but perhaps it was the site of a much earlier monastery or a resting place for monks en route elsewhere?

The Ghost Who Liked to Serve Morning Tea

In his book *Our Haunted Kingdom*, published in 1973, A. Green recalls the curious story of the Richardsons, who once ran a guesthouse in Wyke Gardens. Whilst on business in the Worthing area in August 1951, Mr Green decided to see if his wartime friends, the Richardsons, still ran the guesthouse but discovered they had left years before. As it was now late at night, he decided to take advantage of the 'bed and breakfast' facilities still offered and arranged to stay the night. The next morning at about 8 a.m., Mr Green was awoken by a young lad bringing him a cup of tea. Mr Green noticed that the boy appeared to look ill and had a thin, grey, haggard-looking face and huge saucer-like eyes with dark circles. He thought the child looked miserable and neglected, accentuated by the bedraggled brown suit he was wearing which was far too big for him and hung loosely from his shoulders. He thanked him for the tea but found it to be icy cold and far too sweet for his liking. He looked up to make a comment but the boy had already left the room.

Over the breakfast table Mr Green enquired as to the health of the young boy and was assured that they never provided morning tea for their guests and no children resided in the house. Later an elderly resident guest told Mr Green that a couple of other boarders had experienced similar incidents when sleeping in that particular room. The landlady explained away the half-empty cup of sweetened tea by claiming that it must have been Mr Green's evening refreshment supplied the previous day. Sometime later Mr Green remembered that the Richardsons had told him when he first visited the guesthouse during the war that their eleven-year-old son had been killed in a car crash some five years before. He could not believe that the boy he saw was the Richardsons' son, as they were friendly, generous people who would never have neglected their child. So who was this mysterious young boy and why should he bring guests cups of tea? Perhaps to solve the mystery the history of the building needs to be explored in greater depth.

Worthing's Weeping Angel

A most unusual supernatural story began to unfold in Worthing in 1961 and was reported periodically in the local papers until 1967. It all began when Mr Richard Graves found a Victorian painting lying on the floor of a derelict flat above the garage of a house he had recently moved into at Chichester Road. The picture, which measured 16in by 20in, was a print by an unsigned artist. Its pale colours depicted a winter scene in ancient Palestine, with flights of angels hovering above a shepherd minding his sheep on a hillside in Bethlehem, lit by a single star. Mr Graves, who was a property developer and businessman, picked up the painting when he noticed that one of the angels appeared to be weeping. He carried the painting downstairs to put it in the bin and found a man wandering around the garage. It was getting dark and he wondered what the man wanted, so he proceeded to 'see him off' his premises.

The early 1960s was the time of the 'Flower People'; those who had long hair, colourful caftans and open sandals. The intruder, it would seem, had stepped right out of this scene and, ignoring the garage owner's protests, he tried to grab the picture pleading, 'Don't destroy the picture'. Mr Graves was surprised by this unusual request from a total stranger, then suddenly the picture burst into flames, burning Mr Graves' arm as he dropped it to the floor. At the same moment, the man 'glowed with light' and vanished into thin air. Mr Graves, understandably terrified, ran into the house to find something to treat his burns. After he had recovered from the shock he returned to the garage to find the picture scorched and blackened. He took it into the house to show his wife and left the damaged picture on the kitchen floor, leaning against the wall.

The next morning Mr and Mrs Graves found, to their utter amazement, that the badly damaged painting had somehow been fully restored to its original condition. Another shock awaited the couple later that morning when they noticed a strange pool of water on the tiled kitchen floor. They took a closer look at the painting, thinking that it must have somehow got wet, and noticed that a tear trickled down the surface of the restored painting from one of the eyes of the most prominent angel in the painting. To the couple's bewilderment, the tears continued to flow. They decided to place the picture on one side of the fireplace in the lounge, then on the other, but despite the warmth the angel's eyes still expressed tears. By now Mr and Mrs Graves decided that this strange event was worth investigating further. Within a week, the 'Weeping Angel of Worthing' had made her debut and as news spread through the media it seemed as if the whole world was arriving to have a closer look at the painting.

The Graves' home and privacy was being invaded but they felt compelled to go along with it. They balanced the picture on the bucket in the lounge and allowed the continual stream of visitors to come in and watch the steady flow of the angel's tears. Most visitors recognised these as tears of joy, rather than of sorrow. People soon began bringing little bottles to fill up with water to take home for blessing or healing purposes. These 'free samples' encouraged sick or disabled people to treat the 'open house' as an offshoot of Lourdes. The local churchmen and doctors of various knowledgeable professions came along to view this phenomenon, then, for some unexplained reason, the angel suddenly stopped obliging. The flow of tears lessened to a trickle and finally ceased altogether, much to the relief of the Graves who were pleased to see that the novelty had worn off and the public interest had quickly disappeared.

Time passed and the fuss died down, but several unexplained things happened in the garage to ensure that the intrusions into the property developer's daily life were not over yet. The intruder continued to make an appearance, and made several attempts to catch the eye of Richard Graves by appearing and disappearing in front of him and moving objects from one place to another, but to no avail. Richard was not going to give up easily. One day he did manage to 'get through' to Mr Graves without having to resort to any further alarming performances, and Mr Graves got a full view of the man. According to him, the man was tall with a nondescript face, which was long and hollow-cheeked and bore an expression that he could only define as 'serene and compassionate'. Sometimes the ghost-like intruder appeared as a real person, passing through an open door and closing it behind him, and other times as an apparition, appearing and disappearing at will. As the apparition of the stranger became more common, they were able to enjoy each other's company a little more and gradually, it seems, a rapport began to form between the two. Whilst Mr Graves' own feelings for his new friend became more friendly, the man who had been described as having a 'typical Jesus' face never introduced himself. The ghost remained very much a biblical figure, wearing a long, dark red robe over a white under vesture with a thrown-back hood, revealing his lean features. He had grey eyes, a sparse sandy coloured beard and his hair was long with wiry curls about the forehead and temples. The hands were large with long fingers, and Mr Graves described them as the hands of a craftsman.

Mr Graves had always been well known for his fiery wit and dry sense of humour and by this time he had given his ghostly friend a name, calling him 'Mr Knowall'. One day, the supernatural figure revealed to Mr Graves that the reason for his visitation was to bring his 'message of love to mankind' and to give people a glimmer into what he represented. This bore an unmistakable resemblance to the Sermon on the Mount, found in the Bible's New Testament. Mr Knowall spoke in modern English about a spaceship landing in Russia and of the tremendous changes to come and of much tribulation and catastrophic events. Through it all, Mr Knowall was eager that universal links should be formed around the world, as well as a chain of love to unite all.

Mr and Mrs Graves eventually moved but whatever happened to the painting? Apparently a drop of the salty tears was taken away by a museum official for analysis but there seems to be no report on the outcome. According to a folklorist the picture eventually ended up at the Findhorn Foundation in Morayshire, a spiritual community, eco-village and an international centre for holistic education, where is it greatly revered. Did the town of Worthing receive a visit from a holy man? If so, why was the town chosen?

A Saucy Spirit and a Spate of Spooks

A report appeared in the *Evening Argus* on 30 August 1979 claiming that a vicar blamed spiritualists for a spate of eerie incidents that had put fear into the residents of Worthing, who said they had been haunted by things that go bump in the night. The vicar and the residents put it down to strange goings-on at the spiritualist church, which is situated next door to Christ Church, with a road and the 100-year-old graveyard sandwiched between the two. The vicar, Revd Philip Walton, thought that the spiritualists tuning into medium waves were 'messing with the spirits across the road'. The first incident came to light when an elderly widow with her two children visited him prior to leaving the area. She told the vicar that she had felt a spirit had invaded her privacy by breaking into her bedroom, kissing her and climbing into her bed! Other people who came to her house and stayed in the room had the same spooky experience. The lady tracked down the previous occupants of the house and they also confirmed they had suffered the same experience.

The second incident involved a married lady who was a member of the spiritualist church. She told the vicar that her husband showed a 'Jekyll and Hyde' personality and it appeared there were many things in his life that simply did not add up. She felt that her husband was being taken over by the influence of outside forces. The couple ended up separating. Another incident concerned a young couple who asked the vicar to call at their home as they were hearing strange voices and it sounded like objects were being moved in the night. The vicar read the Litany, one of the most ancient prayers of the Church, at their home and this seemed to quell the unrest for about six or seven weeks, but then the couple left for no apparent reason.

The Revd Walton believed the unnatural events were caused by spirits being disturbed, although he had never personally experienced anything supernatural despite spending many nights at the church. A spiritualist, Mr Raymond Hodges-Paul, dismissed the allegations as 'farcical', insisting strange happenings were nothing new, and believers in spiritualism do not call up spirits nor have ghosts wandering around. He suggested that these mistaken views were through people not understanding the church, and perhaps the incidents could have been imagined because of people's emotional state at the time.

The two churches side-by-side in Grafton Road.

Who or what disturbed those resting in this cemetery?

Strange Goings-On in MGM House

In his book *Haunted Sussex Today*, Andrew Green relates a rather strange occurrence at MGM House in Heene Road, Worthing. This was once the site of West Worthing Assembly Rooms, a Gothic complex that included a baths and skating ring. It was designed in 1865 by G.A. Dean for the new town of West Worthing. A small waterworks was added on the north side of the baths and this provided emergency supplies during the town's typhoid outbreak in 1893. The site later became the Heene Road Swimming Baths and remained in use until 1968 before being demolished in 1973. The present building was opened in September 1996 by the then Heritage Secretary, Virginia Bottomley, when she unveiled a plaque to commemorate the occasion. It would seem that the new office block, headquarters of MGM Assurance (Marine and General Mutual Life Assurance Society), inherited not only the site but also some ghostly residents. Over the years several members of staff have heard mysterious and inexplicable sounds, and two reported the strange feeling of someone's hands resting on their shoulders. Another heard her name being called, although at the time the office was completely empty. A computer also malfunctioned, and for some unexplained reason the screen kept showing the date of 1 January 1904. What is significant about this date? Despite research this date remains a mystery, as no one has been able to find a connection, but the answer must be associated with the previous building.

Why did the computer malfunction at MGM House?

A Midsummer Rendezvous at Broadwater

Broadwater is now within the Borough of Worthing, but the original parish had three settlements, Broadwater village, Offington and Worthing. With the development of Worthing as a seaside resort around 1789, Broadwater became absorbed into the town, with Offington becoming part of the Borough of Worthing in 1902. Broadwater was once a little fishing hamlet with a tidal inlet, hence the name, and it is possible that a port existed near the village in medieval times. It is centred around a large, triangular grassy area known as Broadwater Green, traditionally a site for local fairs and markets, and where during the year various events and activities, such as cricket and the July Broadwater Festival, are held.

The Green is also associated with a macabre tale concerning a group of skeletons who appear to rise from the roots of an old oak tree on Midsummer Eve and dance hand in hand around the tree until dawn or until the first cock crows before sinking back into the ground. Mrs Charlotte Latham, writing in 1868 in a book entitled *Some West Sussex Superstitions*, mentioned one young man who had been unavoidably detained at Findon until late on Midsummer's Eve who passed through Broadwater Green and was 'frightened out of his very senses' when he saw the skeletons capering around the tree. The old oak, known as the Midsummer Tree, is said to be around 300 years old and today this tree is now isolated from the rest of the green on a small triangle of land in the middle of a busy road junction, so if any spirit dancers wish to join in on Midsummer Eve they may have a difficulty reaching their meeting point with today's traffic.

Right: *Broadwater's Midsummer Tree, where on Midsummer's Eve you may see dancing skeletons.*

Below: *A plaque by the tree telling its story.*

Strange Experiences on the Path

Not far from the Green is St Mary's, the parish church of Broadwater, which has an interesting history that dates back to the Domesday survey, although not much of the original Saxon building remains. In April 2005 three local people were walking through the churchyard and suddenly felt a 'tugging' from behind. Two of the group began to feel nauseous and had to leave the churchyard, but one of them decided to return later and felt nothing unusual.

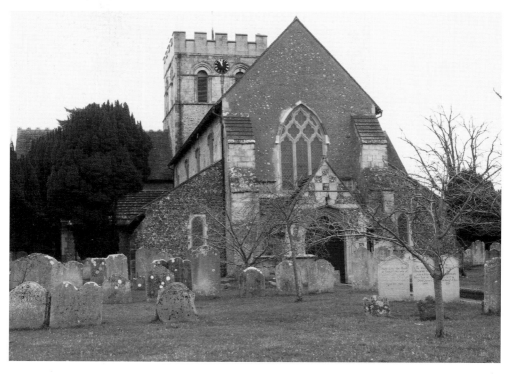

Above: *St Mary's Church, Broadwater, dates back to the Domesday survey, but little of the Saxon church remains.*

Left: *The path through the churchyard where ladies felt someone tugging at them from behind.*

Another view of the path.

A Tunnel Guarded by Supernatural Snakes

At one time Offington Hall was well known for its beautiful manor house which had survived from medieval times, but like many ancient buildings around Worthing it was demolished in the name of development to make way for the Warren roundabout in 1963. It was originally a manor held by Earl Godwin before the Norman Conquest and was owned in the thirteenth century by Thomas de Offington. 'Offington', meaning 'Offa's farmstead', suggests some association with King Offa of Mercia. However, there is no written evidence to prove this, although it is possible that Offa did take control of the Kingdom of Sussex sometime in the eighth century. Offington Manor must have been a spectacular place, as it was recorded that between the twelfth and fifteenth centuries it had grown into a large compound of buildings, which included at least one courtyard, a chapel, a guesthouse and a gatehouse.

It is documented that in 1524 thirty-two household servants lived at the Hall. Thomas West, Lord de la Warr (d. 1554) seems to have made some of the alterations, and by the date of his death the house contained sixty-eight rooms, including the chapel, fifteen storerooms, two halls and three galleries. Twenty-five hearths were recorded in 1664. By 1780 the house had been rebuilt on a much smaller scale, incorporating parts of the earlier building, and consisted of two storeys with two protruding wings on the east front which were built of stone. The house was again repaired and enlarged in 1838.

Twenty years later it was sold, along with an area known as the Park, to Thomas Gaisford for £12,000. He added a new wing on the west front, a library and a chapel, which between 1859 and 1862 was Worthing's chief place of Roman Catholic worship. It was during the 1860s that the Hall and Cissbury Ring became connected in more ways than one. It is claimed that there was a blocked-up tunnel running from behind the panelling in the library to the cellars and then on from Offington Hall to Cissbury Ring, some two miles away. Legend informs us that an enormous fortune in gold treasure was hidden by the ancient peoples who once occupied Cissbury Ring which was guarded by supernatural snakes. The owner of the Hall offered to pay for an excavation, with half any money found being given to whoever would clear out the tunnel and reach the treasure. Several people began digging in earnest, and set about the back-breaking task of clearing the blocked tunnel with pickaxes and shovels. It is not recorded for how long they worked, or how far through the tunnel they went, but some say as they neared the very end of the tunnel they were all driven back by huge snakes that came slithering towards them hissing. The men, fearing they would be bitten by the venomous snakes, retreated and were chased back down the tunnel.

The alleged existence of the subterranean tunnel is remembered by the people of Worthing even though the Hall is now demolished. When Thomas died in 1898 his son, Julian, inherited the estate but decided to leave Offington Hall and take up residence in Dublin on an estate he had inherited from his uncle. The last occupant was Lady de Gex, who moved into the building in 1914. She was the widow of an eminent Victorian QC, Sir John de Gex, who died in 1887. They had been married in 1880 when she was thirty-four and he was seventy-one. Lady de Gex was therefore already sixty-eight when she moved to Offington and always maintained a Victorian lifestyle, dressing in the Victorian fashion. She used a carriage and coachman as her means of transport and was probably the last person in Worthing to own such a vehicle, which could often be seen around the town. The rumours of the secret passage leading from the cellars out to Cissbury Ring were known to Lady de Gex's staff, and despite her reassurances that they had been blocked off many years ago her maids were terrified and refused to enter the cellars. After Lady de Gex moved to Havant in 1935, the house was converted into flats and remained so until it was demolished in 1963.

A Ghost with a Passion for Stroking Hair

At one time Worthing had many windmills, but with the arrival of imported flour and cheaper grain their use declined and now only the one at High Salvington remains. The earliest record of a windmill at Worthing is a reference to a Furlong Mill in East Field in 1616 and again in 1635. In 1831 James Sheppard built a state-of-the-art five-storey windmill with two working stones west of Ham Road, or Ham Lane as it was called in those days, just about opposite to where the closed Half Brick public house stands today. At that time Ham Lane extended into the road which was later renamed Dominion Road. A red-bricked windmill with an octagonal structure, rare in Sussex, was also constructed between 1800 and 1813 for Richard Hide. James Sheppard lived in a cottage close to the mills and the mill continued in use until the last owner, William Baker died in 1896. The south windmill became known as Newland's Navarino Mill, and later the name Navarino was used for both mills. It is believed that they were named after the Battle of Navarino, which took place on 20 October 1827 and was the last fleet action fought solely under sail during the Greek War of Independence, when the combined British, French and Russian fleet defeated the Turkish-Egyptian fleet. Why the mills were so named remains a mystery, but as windmills sweeps are often called sails, this could be the reason.

The mills were eventually demolished in 1909, but the two cottages remained and around 1940 were converted into a single dwelling with two staircases. The lounge and dining room faced east, and the kitchen was extended to the full length of the other two rooms and faced west, occupying the dividing line between the two cottages. There was an interior

Pen and ink drawing by Arthur Elliot showing the miller's house and the Navarino Mills, c. 1885. The ghost here enjoyed stroking hair.

window between the kitchen and the lounge, and the wall below the window was around 3.5ft in height. In the 1990s a couple moved into the cottage with their children and soon became aware of a ghostly presence, which appeared as a person's head and shoulders through the window between the kitchen and the lounge. The spirit was believed to be female because it was small framed and wore a light or grey veil or head covering, which hung down behind the head. The habitual route of the ghost never varied, walking from the north side of the cottage to the south at dusk or during the evening. The couple's thirteen-year-old daughter was sometimes woken in the night with her hair being stroked by an unseen hand. At first her parents did not believe her and put it down to an overactive imagination. However, some years later the couple met the former occupants of the cottage and were asked if the hair-stroking ghost was still active. The couple were astonished, but naturally their daughter was delighted that she had been right all the time, and revealed that the hair stoking had gone on for many weeks. It transpired that the former occupants' own thirteen-year-old daughter had said to her mother one day, 'That was nice what you did last night, Mum, sitting on my bed and stroking my hair!' Who is the mystery ghost and what is the connection with the stroking of hair? Did a former occupant sit with an ailing child and repeat this action, or is it just a spirit with a passion for smoothing hair?

2

West of Worthing

West Tarring

West Tarring, situated just over a mile north-west of Worthing, was once a village, and was less commonly known as Tarring Peverell to set it apart from Tarring Neville, near Lewes. Tarring is mentioned in the Domesday survey as 'Terringes' and the name is thought to have derived from a Saxon ruler, Teorra, meaning 'the place of Teorra's people'.

The Resident at Parsonage Row

West Tarring was granted to Christ Church, Canterbury, by King Athelstan (AD 895-940) and legend informs us that the village was visited by Thomas à Becket in the twelfth century and that he is credited with introducing figs to the village. Whatever the truth, by 1745 an orchard was established from the Old Palace garden cuttings and by 1830 there

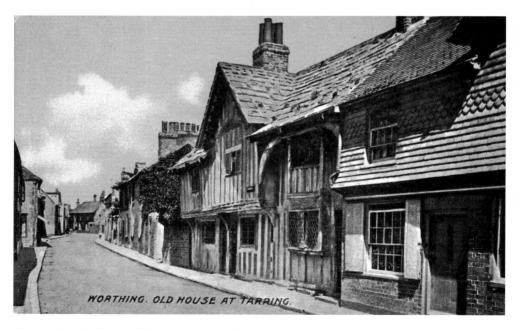

Parsonage Row, High Street, West Tarring, c. 1905. The 500th anniversary celebrations upset the ghost!

were 100 trees yielding about 2,000 dozen figs annually. It became a tourist attraction when a tea garden was opened and a postal delivery service of 'ripe' figs was offered to anywhere in the kingdom. West Tarring is noted for its thirteenth-century parish church, Archbishop's Palace, and numerous old houses, including an excellent example of a fifteenth-century timbered-framed building divided into several cottages at Parsonage Row. They are unique and are the oldest inhabited dwellings in the Borough of Worthing, having been saved from demolition when they were bought by the Sussex Archaeological Trust and restored in July 1963 with the help of a grant of £1,750 from Worthing Council.

In May 1970 the custodian of the cottages decided to hold a party to celebrate the 500th anniversary of the buildings, but the resident poltergeist had other ideas. He obviously did not approve of such celebrations, because he showed his displeasure by opening and slamming doors and windows, and walking unseen backwards and forwards in an empty bedroom. To make his point more clear, a few months earlier he had carefully placed a fourteenth-century charter on the floor and proceeded to throw the easel into a corridor. Today it is claimed the spirit sits on a chair in one of the buildings, but it would appear he is happy with the restorations as he no longer bothers anyone.

Goring-by-Sea

Two miles west of Worthing town centre sits Goring-by-Sea, which is thought to have been the inspiration for the name of the character Lord Goring in Oscar Wilde's play *An Ideal Husband*. For a few years in the 1980s Goring-by-Sea was also the home of the punk rock star Billy Idol (real name William Broad), and Peter Townshend of The Who recorded the beach sounds for the band's album 'Quadrophenia' on the beach at Goring. The word 'Goring' is believed to mean either 'Gara's people' or 'people of the wedge-shaped strip of land', and since 1929 it has been part of the Borough of Worthing. Goring has a long and interesting history, but it also has more than its fair share of ghostly happenings, although none of the ghosts appear to trouble the residents and some even speak fondly of them.

Only Visible to Horses?
In the days before Goring-by-Sea became built up, it was linked to Worthing by a road that was little more than a country lane, bordered by high hedges and elm trees. On the north side of the road was a barn from which seemed to come a power that, in the night, terrified every passing horse. Horses that had to pass by the barn would always swerve to the furthest side of the road, and some say that at midnight the horses would not pass the spot at all. One family recalled a story of how whilst being driven homewards their horse absolutely refused to pass by the barn. Finally, after much coaxing, they had to admit defeat and give up on the attempt to reach home, which was less than a quarter of a mile away. Instead they had to turn back to the Worthing end of the road and go home via a route which was three to four miles longer. The landscape is now very different, with the rural lane having been replaced by a wide tarmac road which is bordered by modern houses, but I wonder if any horse having to travel this road at night today would hesitate or stop where the barn once stood?

Major William Lyon of Goring Hall

An interesting incident of a supernatural nature occurred on the evening of 30 December 1925, and also appeared in the *Worthing Herald*. It seems that two of Goring's residents, George Lewis and his wife, were walking home after enjoying an evening at the Downsview Inn in West Worthing. As they were walking back to their home at No. 2 The Crib, Sea Lane, down Goring Lane, Mrs Lewis turned to her husband and asked him if he could see an apparition of an angel going down the road ahead of them. Mr Lewis laughed loudly and blamed the whole incident on an enjoyable night out at the public house and an overactive imagination. However, as they came into the village Mrs Lewis again insisted she could see an angel and watched it continue on through the lodge gates of Goring Hall and disappear into the avenue of ilex trees. Before returning home, they called in on one of their neighbours, the Prescotts, who lived at No. 4, but they too did not believe her and the shrieks of laughter coming from downstairs soon woke the Prescott children as Mrs Lewis tried to convince everyone of what she had seen.

The next morning the village woke to the sad news that Major William Lyon of Goring Hall had died the previous night, just before midnight, at about the same time as Mrs Lewis had seen the angel. This story is also told by Frank Fox-Wilson in his book *The Story of Goring and Highdown*. It was related to him by Mervyn Prescott, who was one of the children and at the time the book was written in 1972 was in his seventies.

The thatched cottages called The Crib, Sea Lane, Goring in 1925. Bungalows were later built on this site.

The Phantom Ghost who Liked Jumping Out at People

From the same era, there is another story of an incident that took place in December 1929. The story claimed that local workman Morris Jenkins was 'scared out of his wits' by a terrifying apparition near Goring Hall on a cold winter's day. He could not have imagined the alarm and concern his sighting would raise amongst the villagers of Goring and Ferring. In the days that followed, numerous local villagers were also shocked by an apparition that kept jumping out and frightening people, and soon speculation about a local ghost reached a new height. The vicar of Ferring, Revd S.M. Morgan, joined in by giving a stern warning from the pulpit. 'If somebody has conjured up the ghost as a joke, it had now gone beyond a laughing matter'. He went on to say that if the ghost was seen by anyone, then 'such spectres are not protected by law', and emphasised, in what seemed like an unchristian manner, that he 'would welcome news that the apparition had been brought to heel'.

The next day, the father of Morris Jenkins told a sceptical *Worthing Herald* reporter:

My son first saw the ghost when he was walking home from work. He arrived home very agitated and explained that he was halfway along Goring Hall Drive when he was confronted by something in white. He swished his arm at it then ran the rest of the way home.

A second youth, George Sopp, who was one of Morris's neighbours, declared that he had also seen the ghost in the same place when cycling along Goring Hall Drive. George told his mother that the apparition popped up from the bushes at the side of the road and that he was so frightened he almost fell off; the next moment the ghost had floated off across the fields.

Days after the ghostly sighting by Morris Jenkins, a report on the nocturnal apparition appeared in the *Worthing Herald* and during the following week the spirit in white appeared on consecutive nights in the neighbourhood of Goring Hall Drive. People living near the cricket ground behind the Bull's Head saw a white figure moving across the grass at night, as though dancing on the Goring cricket pitch, and also in Bull Fields. Harold, the railway ticket office clerk, tried to solve the mystery, and one night he dressed up as a woman and wandered around the area for hours, but without any success of a sighting. By now the men and youths of the village had banded together and were scouring Ferring and Goring armed with pitchforks, cudgels and other weapons. One man even turned out with a sporting gun! As most sightings were reported in the vicinity of Goring Hall Drive, the self-styled 'ghost vigilantes' laid in wait in this area for several nights, hoping the apparition would reappear. However, it didn't oblige. It later transpired that that the 'ghost' was none other than an odd chap with the appropriate name of Mr Nutter, who cycled over from his home in Grand Avenue, Worthing, put a white sheet over his head and danced around the cricket pitch.

Does the Landlord Still Haunt the Bull Inn?

Parts of the Bull Inn in Goring Street, Goring, date back to the sixteenth century and some of the original walls are nearly 1m thick. At one time Goring Street was the only road in the village and led down to Goring Hall. The inn was originally known as the Bull's Head, and the original Bull's Head sign, described in 1927 as portraying 'a hefty ferocious beast' with its head inclined slightly to one side as though watching everyone with suspicion, was, despite local protests, removed by the brewery in the 1970s and given to a pub in East Sussex. The date of the original building is unknown but during renovations in the 1970s to open up an entrance between the inglenook and the main bars, two Tudor windows on either side of the old front door were revealed. We can only surmise that they were bricked up to avoid window tax. The Bull's Head, like many old inns, doubled up as the village mortuary to store the dead prior to burial taking place, as the taproom was often the coolest place in the village. Often the makeshift mortuary would contain the bodies of unknown sailors washed up on the nearby beach.

These inns were also used as a venue for inquests, and one in 1890 about a boating fatality affected the jury and witnesses so strongly that they decided to give their fees – which amounted to 18s, a good sum in those days – to the woman who had just been widowed.

An unusual inquest took place in the summer of 1907 into the tragic deaths of two young men, Sidney Orchard, aged nineteen, and Fredrick Wadey, aged twenty-two, who had been killed on Highdown by a bolt of lightning. The accident happened near the Lodge House whilst they were sheltering under an old elm tree with Sidney's father and Arthur Winton. The two young men were killed instantly, Arthur was seriously injured and Sidney's father stunned. At the inquest it was revealed that the men's boots had been torn to shreds and the nails in Sidney's boots driven into his feet. Their clothes were also torn to

The Bull's Head, Goring. Does a former landlord still haunt this pub?

shreds and coins from Sidney's pockets were found embedded in the ground, with a penny and halfpenny fused together.

In an inn as old as the Bull it is not surprising to learn of a ghost, although some say in this instance there are at least three. One would appear to be very punctual, as at precisely 6.50 p.m. he can be heard walking across the floor above the bar. However, one landlord dismissed the ghost theory, favouring an explanation that it was simply the sound of hot water pipes trying to cope with an air lock, although why it should happen at precisely the same time every day is a mystery. This did not explain the bottles that would fall off the shelves late at night when the staff were locking up. Local residents also report that a male ghost has been seen. He is in shirtsleeves and wears braces to hold up his trousers. It seems that a one-time landlord met his end by falling down the stairs and breaking his neck, and one can only wonder if this is the ghost of the landlord who met his end so abruptly.

Mr Frank Fox-Wilson mentions a villager, Alexander Robinson, in his book, who recorded a number of village ghosts, of whom one visited the old vicarage in Jefferies Lane. Apparently the occupants were 'well accustomed' to hearing their ghost opening the front door and mounting the stairs. The spirit clattered dishes in the kitchen, but was rarely seen until it developed the habit of sitting on people's beds in the form of a lady, referred to by some of the older villagers as the Grey Lady. Was this one ghost or two? Robinson also describes another 'little old lady' who used to visit the Court House when the Barclay-Watson sisters lived there. This ghost had the habit of peering over their gate from time to time, and Robinson suggests that it may be something to do with the old gravestone that had been used as a paving stone at the Court House entrance. An examination of the stone revealed it had not come from the grave of an old lady, but of a boy named Thomas Holcombe who had died in 1730. Perhaps the ghost was his mother or grandmother who wanted to see her son or grandson's grave intact once more?

Highdown Hill

Highdown Hill is a spectacular hill on the South Downs that straddles the Borough of Worthing and Arun district. It started life as a late Bronze Age enclosure, and was replaced by a hill fort in the Iron Age period. However, it is noted for its Anglo-Saxon cemetery, created in AD 450 and has produced a number of unusual glass objects, which can be seen in Worthing Museum. Today it is a popular venue for walkers, dog-walkers and picnickers. It overlooks the areas of Littlehampton, Angmering, Ferring and Worthing, with excellent views in good weather as far as Seven Sisters in the east and the Isle of Wight in the west. It now belongings to the National Trust.

Miller's Tomb

Goring's most eccentric and famous character must be John Olliver, who was an eighteenth-century miller and poet. There are so many mysteries surrounding him that it is hard to distinguish fact from fiction. He was reputed to have been a smuggler and used his mill for signalling the all-clear to ships arriving with illicit goods. What we do know is that in 1765, at the age of fifty, he began building his own tomb on Highdown Hill, which was owned by William Westbrooke Richardson. The land had once been the site of an Iron Age camp, a Roman bath house and a pagan Saxon cemetery. Olliver is alleged to have visited the tomb every day, where he would sit and meditate with his Bible on his knees. The inscription on the tomb lid is dated 1766, confirming that it was built twenty-seven years before he died. Legend informs us that if you run around his tomb twelve times at midnight, John Olliver's ghost will jump out of the tomb and chase you. The tomb is elaborately engraved with many verses, although most are now very worn and unreadable. One of the verses he penned is as follows:

> My tomb on a lofty hill doth stand,
> Where I sit and view both sea and land;
> With iron palisades I am surrounded in,
> The expense of it I value not a pin.
> For in my own works I take great delight,
> And praise my MAKER day and night;
> When death doth call then I must go
> With him whether I would or no,
> And leave my mill and all behind,
> In hopes a better place to find.

It is said that John Olliver was buried upside down because he believed that at the Last Judgement the world would turn 'topsy-turvy' and when it happened he wanted to be the first to be facing the right way.

John Olliver had been born in Lancing in 1709 and worked the old mill there before moving to Goring. In 1750 he took over Highdown Mill from his father, Clement Olliver,

The miller's tomb in 1907, showing the inscriptions.

The miller's tomb in 2010. Most of the inscriptions are now unreadable.

and prior to building his tomb he kept a coffin under his bed so that is was ready for use if he needed it. It is claimed that he had written the following lines on his coffin:

> Beneath my bed my coffin stands,
> On four wheels swift it runs,
> I am always proud to show the same,
> And why my neighbours do you me blame.

It is said that the coffin was used as a hiding place for his smuggled goods, and his spacious tomb on Highdown Hill also stored more of his contraband. Others claim that the verses inscribed around the tomb are elaborate codes revealing where the miller had hidden the proceeds of his illegal activities. When he died his wife established a tea chalet near the tomb which became popular with visitors to Worthing. Sadly, in November 1982 vandals badly damaged the tomb and destroyed many of the inscriptions on it. There is no burial entry in the Goring register for John Olliver, but on 26 January 1812 there is a footnote which reads:

> John Olliver of this Parish, Miller, was buried under the Tomb on High Down Hill, April 26 1793, aged 83. On this occasion the funeral service was read and a sermon preached at the Tomb by Ann Street, a young woman of Goring who used to read to him before his death, his eyesight having become defective.

His funeral drew a crowd of thousands and his body was brought from his house in a white-painted coffin followed by young maidens all dressed in white and carried around

Close-up of the skeleton on one end of the miller's tomb on Highdown Hill, still clearly visible today.

the field. The sermon, read by his granddaughter Ann Street, was said to have been written by John himself, but it was actually taken from a printed volume of sermons written by the Church of England clergy.

A more recent haunting was reported in the *Worthing Gazette and Herald* on 29 July 1983. Two schoolboys from Durrington High School reported to the local press that they were camping on Highdown Hill and had heard the story about running around the tomb twelve times, so set their alarms and at midnight actually ran around the tomb. Nothing happened, but as they were walking away they heard footsteps and turned to see the ghost of John Olliver. One of the lads was only 10yds away and said, 'He was a very old man with a pale face, and I think he had a moustache. He was losing his hair and was very short'. Whatever the truth we will never know, but Highdown Hill continues to be a favourite spot for families to picnic and the tales of John Olliver will live on.

East Preston

East Preston was once a thriving farming community dating back to 1087. It is known as the village by the sea, and includes the Angmering-by-Sea Estate which joins the foreshore and borders open farmland to the east. It still retains much of its old character.

A Spooky Picture is Spirited Away from a Pub

An interesting story was printed in the *Evening Argus* on 9 July 1976 concerning a macabre drawing that had mysteriously vanished from a village pub in East Preston. Two legends are told; the first concerns the villagers who feared the soul of a dead criminal or a suicide victim (he is referred to as either depending on which legend you are reading). The villagers pinned his body to the ground with a heavy millstone and thrust a wooden stake through his heart, believing his ghost would not be able to get up and haunt anyone. They then buried the poor soul at the then lonely crossroads.

The second legend states that a millstone broke loose and rolled down from Highdown Hill, killing a man who was walking on the Worthing road. Reports suggest that, as no one could lift it, earth was piled on top of the man and the millstone. Others claim the

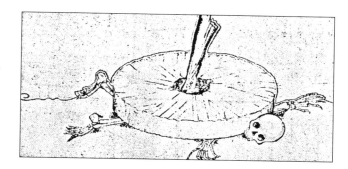

Right: Spooky drawing depicting the story of the millstone. Did someone steal this drawing or was it spirited away?

Below: Roundstone in 2010. It is now a Premier Inn.

millstone lay on the grass by the crossroad at the southern end of the lane, roughly where the level crossing is today, but had disappeared by the twentieth century. We are not told if these drastic measures proved effective in laying the ghost, but the Roundstone public house was opened in 1939 and obviously got its name from these tales. During the 1960s the sign outside the pub showed a skeleton struggling to lift a millstone.

In 1973 the Roundstone pub was taken over by Mr and Mrs Fry, who had been the licensees at the Harrow in Cheam. Prior to taking over the pub Mr Fry and his wife had called into the Roundstone for a drink. During this visit they told the legend of the Roundstone to an artist who happened to be in the pub at the time. The artist was so inspired that he drew a scene showing a tortured skeleton pinned down by a grey millstone and fixed by a brown wooden stake against a black background. The drawing was given to Mr and Mrs Fry when they moved in and was screwed to the hallway wall above the glass doors of the Millstone Bar, where it remained until the spooky painting disappeared in July 1976, despite it being in view while customers were being served. Mr and Mrs Fry could not explain its disappearance, and said it was eerie as they would have been able to see any movement behind the doors and still they did not glimpse a thing being taken. 'We cannot put a value on the picture,' said Mr Fry, 'I do not believe it was taken by a ghost but I would like to catch the phantom that slipped in and stole it'. Was the painting spirited away or had someone sneaked past and stolen it? No one knows.

Mrs Fry said that she did not believe in ghosts. 'I am not a woman who drinks and I have not got a vivid imagination,' but admits there have been strange goings-on in the pub. Mrs Fry saw the apparition of man in her bedroom when she was suddenly awoken by the mournful howl of her old English sheepdog at 3 a.m. one morning, and although she does not believe in ghosts, in her mind she could clearly see the man. She screamed and the man disappeared. Her husband believed her to be hallucinating until very early one morning, around 6 a.m. he was sitting having a cup of tea by the fireplace in the Millstone Bar when something made him glance up. He saw a man standing behind the bar who then disappeared before his eyes.

Angmering

The village of Angmering, situated about four miles west of Worthing, still retains its rustic charm with some timber-framed buildings that date back to the fourteenth century. Six cottages, known by the unusual name of 'Longback cottages', are protected by a preservation order as buildings of historical interest and were built in 1728 as 'homes of refuge' for the aged poor of the parish. According to local historian Edwin Harris, writing in 1910, the name 'Longback' may have arisen because amongst Sussex labourers the term means to 'straighten the back for a temporary rest', and so retiring people are referred to as 'going in for the longback'. Angmering derives from a Saxon farming settlement of around AD 600, and it is thought that the original name was 'Angenmaering' meaning 'Angenmaer's people'. According to the Domesday Book, 'Angemare' (as it was spelt then) had two manors, possibly those of East and West Angmering. Following the arrival of William of Normandy the manors seem to have been subdivided into five, with

Bargeham (later Barpham), Ham and Ecclesden added. Ecclesden was granted to Roger de Montgomery, who had been created Earl of Arundel in recognition of his services as a divisional commander of the Norman Army at the Battle of Hastings in 1066. In time the manor passed to the Abbey of Fécamp, and then, during the fifteenth century, to the Abbey of Syon. In 1384 Angmering became a town and received a charter to hold a Saturday market and an annual fair. During the fourteenth and fifteenth centuries it continued to prosper, probably because of the quality of the soil and its successful sheep farming. However, by 1840 Angmering's hiring fair had ceased and the small town declined, reverting to village status. With such a rich, eventful history, it is not surprising to learn that there has been numerous strange happenings in and around the village.

Cursed by French Nuns

After the Reformation, Angmering, like many other places, suffered from the changes brought about by Henry VIII. Land which had formally belonged to the Church was sold off to new landowners to pay for the king's mounting debts. Sir John Palmer was a notorious landowner, described locally as 'a man corrupt in conscience', who bought up land at Angmering previously held by the Abbess of Fécamp and drove off the 'copyhand' tenants, destroying their cottages and orchards. The Angmering tenants, John Bune, Thomas Hall, John and Thomas Yonge, Robert Benett and John Attfelld [sic] appealed to the Court of the Star Chamber with a Bill of Complaint as they felt that Sir John had acted unfairly, but they were unsuccessful. However, it would appear that Sir John inherited more than just the land. Local legend states that the French nuns had placed a curse on the Abbey of Fécamp, now known as Ecclesden Manor, when it was previously seized by Edward IV. The curse meant that whilst it was not owned by the French, no male heir would be born in the house. Although Sir John Palmer held the manors of West Angmering and Ecclesden, there is no evidence that he ever lived at Ecclesden. He had at least one child, Sir Thomas Palmer, born in 1543, who had at least nine children of his own. Eccelsden never stayed for long in any one owner's hands, and there is no evidence that a male heir has been born at the manor in the last 400 years. If there has been a male, then it is said that the father has sold the manor before a son could inherit. Perhaps the story of the curse was invented much later to fit the facts? Who knows?

However, in the eighteenth century the manor was bequeathed to James Grant from Poling who had fourteen children, including some males, so maybe there was French blood in the family or perhaps the curse was simply losing its power.

In 1912 the estate was purchased by Walter Butcher, who restored the property and did much for Angmering. Mr Butcher was a great admirer of Marshal Frederick Foch, the French commander of the Allied armies on the Western Front during the First World War, and when Walter Butcher died in 1953 he bequeathed the manor to the Foch family, as Marshal Foch had died in 1929. In his will Walter states:

> By reason of my admiration for the late Marshal Foch and of my feeling that his invaluable services to our Country as well as his own have never been adequately recognised I am anxious to pay an Englishman's tribute to the memory of this great French soldier to whom we all owe so much. I therefore direct that my Trustees shall stand possessed of the capital and

Ecclesdon Manor, with a view across the lawn, 1910.

future income of my trust fund. In trust for all or any the daughters or daughter of Marshal Foch living at my death and the children or child then living of any then deceased daughter of Marshal Foch being male attain the age of twenty one years or being female attain that age or marry under that age and if more than one in equal shares as tenants in common but so that the children or child of any deceased daughter of his shall take (equally between them as tenants in common if more than one) only the share which their his or her mother would have taken had she survived me and attained a vested interest.

Eventually his relatives were traced in France and were puzzled, having no knowledge of Mr Butcher or the manor. The Foch family owned the manor for twelve years and spent their summer months there, but they never actually took up residence. It is said that during their occasional visits they made a rather bizarre sight walking down the High Street to the centre of village, several of them dressed in black. It is interesting to note that in the eleventh century, the manor should have been granted to a Norman Army commander and some 900 years later it was bequeathed to a French Army commander in similar circumstances. Readers interested in the Butchers of Ecclesden Manor can read an extensive article on www.angmeringvillage.co.uk/history/Butchers.htm

Monks at Angmering

I have not been surprised to learn of several sightings of hooded monks in the area covered by this book, because when you look into the history in and around Worthing there are many references to the Knights Templar and pilgrim inns. However, the famous, well-documented sighting of an enormous monk did astound me. Legend informs us that a hooded monk, said to be around 8ft tall, haunts the lane leading from the Spotted Cow public house to Ecclesden Manor and beyond into Highdown Hill. Some say that Ecclesden Manor was at one time a monastery, but there does not seem to be any evidence to prove this. On an August evening in 1964, farm worker Roy Chambers was checking on some cattle grazing in a field when he noticed a monk dressed in a brown habit sitting on a bank reading a prayer book. As Roy approached and came within 3yds of the apparition, the monk rose up to his full height, estimated at 8ft, and dwarfed him. Terrified, Roy ran away as fast as he could but when he looked back the monk had completely vanished. Perhaps this monk was evicted at the time of the Dissolution of the Monasteries from 1536 but decided to stay on in defiance.

Does the Ghost of 'Old Wilkie' still reside at the Lamb Inn?

The Lamb Inn overlooking the Square dates from around 1780 and, like so many buildings in and around Worthing, is now a listed building. Legend claims that the room near the archway leading to the stables was once used as a village mortuary, and later when the roof over this part of the property was being repaired, a small attic room was found which may have been used as overnight accommodation by post-boys or grooms who would have serviced the horse-drawn coaches on a daily basis as they arrived at Angmering. One of the bedrooms above is reputed to be frequented by a 'woman in white'. In 1991, the then landlord, Russell Hall, said he heard footsteps when no one was in the house. Neil Rogers-Davis, who hosts an excellent website on Angmering called Angmering Village Life (www.angmeringvillage. co.uk) told me that in 2005 he was talking to the bar manager and his wife and learned that they had been playing with an Ouija board in the inn with some friends one evening. The board spelled out the words 'the green room'. As none of the rooms have names they were a little puzzled, but dismissed the matter. When Mr Rogers-Davis told them that in the 1920s one of the bedrooms did have that name, the couple went white! Another apparition, of an elderly Victorian-dressed gentleman, has been seen sitting on a stool warming himself near the vast open hearth fireplace in the bar restaurant. This is thought to be the ghost of one of the most colourful landlords, Mr Thomas Wilkinson, known to the locals as 'Old Wilkie'. He came to the Lamb in 1850 and was still there in 1907 when he applied to the magistrates at Arundel for the renewal of his licence at the age of eighty-one!

In 2009 the descendents of Old Wilkie came from all over the country, along with others from as far away as Australia, to hold a reunion at the pub. Later one of the family wrote to Mr Rogers-Davis to relate some eerie experiences to him:

My friend suffered a severe pain in her chest, which she described as if she felt it didn't belong to her, but she had to get out of the pub. After she left it gradually went, but it returned when we had to go in and pick up belongings, and went again when we left. She didn't mention it to me until the day after, although I knew there had been something wrong. Jo felt extremely spooked by being inside, and also very uncomfortable.

The correspondent told Mr Rogers-Davis that he was talking to a couple outside the pub, who said that they had been having a drink inside when one of the menus fell off the counter and went across the room for no apparent reason. He continued, 'I don't know

Is Old Wilkie still making his presence known at the Lamb Inn, Angmering?

if there is a reputation for "goings-on" or whether it was all just coincidence'. None of these people mentioned their experience until someone else mentioned theirs, and it took the family a few days to find out that others had felt something too. The correspondent concluded his letter by writing, 'Given that we are all sane, normal human beings (and you will have to take my word for that!) and not prone to paranoia, it was all very strange'.

Other Recent Experiences in Angmering

There is supposed to be a female ghost at New Place Farm, where only one wing of the old manor house now stands. Also, the ghost of a young child is claimed to have been seen at an attic window at Angmering Manor Hotel, which was previously the old sixteenth-century rectory.

At Angmering's annual village fair in 2006, Mr Rogers-Davis was approached by a young lady who owned a house at the north end of the then newly built Bramley Green development. She asked whether there had previously been a house on the site and whether there had been a murder there. Mr Rogers-Davis replied that there hadn't to his knowledge, and she went on to tell him that her family had experienced several doors flying open and the sound of footsteps without a sign of anyone. Mr Rogers-Davis later established that the house had been built across an ancient footpath that had been closed to the public when the building work had begun. I wonder who this person is who could have been objecting to the new build?

The caretaker of the new Angmering Community Centre (opened in October 2009) at Bramley Green also told Mr Rogers-Davis that he had been unnerved when cleaning the empty building. On several occasions he had heard the sound of footsteps that appeared to cross the main hall in a north to south direction. In January 2010 he experienced another scary incident after a performance in the hall. Long after everyone had left the building and the main doors were locked, he was cleaning up in the kitchen when, from the hall, he heard the sound of an audience applauding. He left the building very quickly! The Community Centre has been built right across yet another ancient footpath, a modern one to replace it being made to the east of the site. Who knows what unseen occurrences will be heard in the ancient village?

Rustington

Just a mile from Angmering is the village of Rustington, but it is far larger than a village and has expanded over the last few years. Within the village is a conservation area containing many Grade II listed buildings. It also has some of the best preserved seventeenth- and eighteenth-century flint cottages in West Sussex, many of which are thatched. On display in the High Street is a large boulder which was brought to Rustington by the sea ice during the Ice Age.

Farewell to 'Dear Rusty'

Rustington, situated just seven miles from Worthing, is a seaside resort and is officially a village with its own parish council, although it is much larger than its status implies. According to the last census the population is over 13,000 and has the facilities of a small town, but it is still a village because its residents voted for it to remain so.

Over the years Rustington has been the home to many famous people, including the prolific composer Hubert Parry. The Parry family came to Rustington in 1876, recommended by a friend because of his wife's health problems. Parry decided to build his own home and chose the architect Norman Shaw to design it. He was heavily involved in the entire process as an army of forty-six skilled craftsmen men worked on the plans. Parry's daughter laid the foundation stone of the house at 'Dear Rusty', as he called Rustington. Parry planned some of the grounds himself, and finally on 22 July 1881 the family moved into their new residence, which they decided to name Knight's Croft. A feast was laid on for the workers.

Their first winter at Rustington was not easy with snow drifts of up to 9ft, but the resourceful Parry made good use of the cold snap by skating on the pond and composing, and when he wasn't busy with this he wrote articles on music. His most popular work is 'Jerusalem', which has now been adopted by the Women's Institute as their hymn. Interestingly the words are supposed to have been penned by William Blake in Felpham, making it a truly Sussex hymn. On completion of the manuscript the modest Parry handed it to Sir Walter Davies with a 'Here's a tune for you'. Parry was made a knight in 1898, which was rather fitting as he so enjoyed living at Knight's Croft.

After contracting Spanish flu during the global pandemic, Sir Hubert died at his home on 7 October 1918. His body was cremated and his ashes placed in the crypt of St Paul's

Cathedral in London. However, Sir Hubert must have found it very hard to leave his house at Dear Rusty as when the new owners of Knight's Croft moved into the house, they were surprised to see a ghost walk straight through the wall. The lady recognised the ghost as Sir Hubert looking his jovial self with his white walrus-style moustache and was not in the least upset or afraid of such a kind old man. In seems that Sir Hubert's ghost took this one last longing look around his dear old home, as if to reassure himself that it was in safe hands, before vanishing, never to be seen again.

Littlehampton

Littlehampton is steeped in history dating back to the Roman period. The Anglo-Saxon village was known as Hampton, and it wasn't until the fourteenth century that it became Little Hampton so that sailors could distinguish it from the much larger Southampton. In 1139 Empress Matilda landed here to begin war with King Stephen. The port was a royal dockyard of Henry VIII and a quay was built in the 1670s. The growth of the port resulted in a new river mouth being cut in 1735, while Littlehampton's Redoubt was built to guard the town and protect the River Arun in the 1750s. Littlehampton used to be the chosen holiday resort of artists and writers, attracted by its peaceful atmosphere compared to larger towns such as Brighton. In particular, Percy Bysshe Shelley and Samuel Taylor Coleridge spent a lot of time here, as well as Lord Byron who stayed at the Dolphin inn between 20 and 30 August 1806 and tethered his horses in stables behind the hotel. He reputedly went for a swim in the river with his Newfoundland dog, Boatswain (Bosun), and nearly drowned!

However, Littlehampton seems to have another claim to fame; the Dolphin Hotel on the corner of the High Street and Surrey Street has been named the most haunted location in West Sussex.

Spooky Goings-On at the Dolphin
The delightful Dolphin has a fascinating history, a welcoming and friendly atmosphere, a well-stocked bar and delicious food, but it also appears to be a portal where numerous ghosts come and go at will. It has been subject to many paranormal investigations, including one by the highly acclaimed Living TV's Derek Acorah and Colin Fry, who said in their filmed visit that the building had many spirits. The original site dates back to 1735, when it was a coaching inn with large stables and three workers' cottages in the grounds. The building then became an olde worlde 'convenience' store serving the people of the town with their needs, and as the local shop was the hub of any community, perhaps this is why so many spirits congregate on this site.

The present Dolphin came about a few years later when two brothers who owned the original Dolphin public house just across the road had a bitter quarrel and one moved into the convenience store, turned it into a pub and called it the Dolphin! Finally, after years of arguing, one of the brothers backed down and the Dolphin we see today kept its name whilst the other pub became the Swan. On Friday 10 March 2010, Worthing and District Paranormal Society (WDPS) named the building the most haunted in West Sussex.

Ellie Boiling, who has run the pub with her partner Katie Smith for the last six years, is passionate about the pub and told the *Littlehampton Gazette* that she was completely overwhelmed by the award.

The Dolphin is also home to LIGHT (Littlehampton Investigative Ghost Hunting Team) which is run by Ellie. When I went along to chat to Ellie and Katie about this amazing building, I didn't expect to experience so much activity for myself. As we chatted

Above: *The Dolphin on the corner of Surrey Street and High Street, Littlehampton, the most haunted place in the town.*

Right: *Ellie and Katie with the award naming the Dolphin Hotel the most haunted building in West Sussex.*

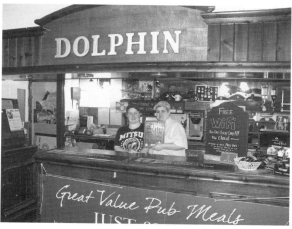

Ellie, who is incredibly enthusiastic about her home and its 'family' of spirits, said there were many incidents to relate. For example, a man came into the pub with a parrot on his shoulder and Ellie told him that no pets were allowed in the pub. He said, 'Well you have a little black and white dog in here!' Several people had noticed the little dog that runs around the bar and then seems to disappear near the pool table. Research has revealed that when Lord Byron visited the pub in 1806 he brought his beloved black and white dog, Boatswain, with him, but two years later it died of rabies when only five years old. Is this Lord Byron's dog?

Ellie then went on to tell me about Room 2. A couple had booked in for a week's holiday and paid in advance. The couple were seen to their room and shortly afterwards the man appeared in the bar wearing only a towel. Ellie told him if he wanted a drink she would bring it to his room, but he couldn't stay in the bar in a state of undress. Apparently he was preparing for bed when an apparition of a woman with no bottom half came through the door and floated out through the window! The following morning the couple had departed, with the CCTV showing them leaving at 4.30 a.m. Ellie has no idea where they would have gone at that early hour. When Ellie telephoned to say she would return their money, the couple would not answer the telephone.

Katie, who was once very sceptical, recalls an experience when she went to clean Room 4 and a shadowy figure of a man passed straight through her. The room has a very strange presence and Ellie recalls the day a priest booked in and was given this room. Moments later he came downstairs requesting to be moved to another immediately as the room had a very bad presence. Research revealed that a man who had been a resident in the room had died of a heart attack, but why he should haunt the room is unclear.

The most eerie room in the building is Room 7, which used to be the children's nursery in the original building. Ellie said she would tell me no more until I visited the room with Katie, as she herself didn't like going in the room. I approached the room with an open mind and was utterly amazed to first experience the rapid change in the temperature. There was an icy breeze slicing through the room and I could feel it swirling around my ankles, and there was certainly a strange atmosphere. As Katie and I talked, we heard footsteps and a loud knocking on the walls. I also heard what sounded to me like a wooden ball being dropped on the floor which then proceeded to 'bump' along the floor making sounds similar to those heard when a game of skittles are being played. Could this have been a wooden child's toy of some kind? I looked around and saw what I can only describe as a white, smoky mist in the left-hand corner of the room rising and gathering into a ball, and then suddenly it was gone.

When I told Katie, she said she had also experienced orbs in this room, with green lights flashing. Downstairs Ellie told me that a young girl, who said her name was Little Dolly, had appeared in this room. In the nursery was a cupboard, and one day they decided to open it and had to prise the door as it has not been opened for many years. Inside they found a broken photographic image of female child, and a whole image of a male child. Ellie pieced together the image of the child and put it away wondering who it might be. Much later Debbie Dean, a medium and spiritualist artist, visited the pub to draw what she saw. In Room 7, in total darkness, she drew a picture of a little girl who, unprompted, she said was a child named Dolly who had died of diphtheria in that room. Ellie then

The broken photographic image of Little Dolly found in cupboard in the nursery where she died.

A drawing by Debbie Dean as she saw Little Dolly, in total darkness, in the nursery.

compared the photographic image she had found with Debbie's drawing and was amazed to see a striking resemblance. Debbie could also see the word 'mummy' or 'memory' in front of the child. One day a man came into the Dolphin and asked if he could have a look around as his grandfather had lived there with his wife and fourteen children. He said one of the children, named Little Dolly, had died of diphtheria. Ellie told him what she had discovered and later the man took her to Littlehampton cemetery to show her the grave of Little Dolly, her name clearly visible on the tomb. Apparently the building is full of spirited, lively children, whom Ellie says can be quite mischievous at times, opening and closing doors or running along the corridors on the third floor.

I was then taken on a tour of the cellar. Although cellars are always cold, there was a distinct icy breeze blowing through the room as well as a haunting eeriness. Ellie explained that the spirit of an old blacksmith, Frederick, resides in the cellars which at one time used to be the stables. When Debbie Dean visited she sat in the cellar, in darkness, and drew Frederick, as well as other ghosts that haunt the Dolphin. There has also been the sound of gunshot heard in the cellars and the strong smell of sulphur. There is a dividing wall that was added at some time and Ellie told me that on occasions there has been a horrible smell, like rotten flesh, coming from behind it. Mediums have staked their reputation on the fact that there is a dead body behind the wall!

The Dolphin, like other parts of Littlehampton, has a bricked-up tunnel in its cellar that is believed to be linked to the days of smuggling along the river. Local legend informs us that at one time these tunnels collapsed and someone was crushed to death, so they were bricked up permanently. This could explain why there is so much activity in the small area from the corner of the High Street and along Surrey Street. When we walked

Drawing of the blacksmith, Frederick, who resides in the cellar, as Debbie Dean saw him.

to the area where the tunnel had been Ellie asked the spirits to let us know they were there. Suddenly I felt something hit the lower part of my leg, like someone stabbing me or flicking a finger at me. It didn't hurt, but the sting was real. I wonder whether this one of the children having some fun?

Back upstairs, in the warmth of the bar, Ellie told me that one medium who visited the ladies' toilet came back and said she had seen someone rolling out pastry in the toilet! Investigation revealed that the kitchen was once located in this area and that a worker, Jane, had been murdered by her uncle William.

The nursery at the Dolphin Hotel, where an icy cold slices through you, strange sounds are heard and orbs are seen.

Recently Ellie and Katie said they have had 20p coins falling from the ceiling and, on one occasion, a handful was thrown across the room and a female customer was hit on the chest, the impact leaving a mark on her skin. The Dolphin also has an extensive collection of Elvis Presley, *Titanic* and First and Second World War memorabilia. Ellie said she has seen the spirit of an airman standing near this display, so is he recalling his contribution to the war?

The bricked-up wall in the cellar, behind which mediums say a body is buried.

The corridor leading to the blocked-up tunnel which collapsed. This area has a very spooky feeling!

Second World War memorabilia, where a ghostly airman has been seen looking at the display.

A customer sitting at the bar recalled the time when there was a celebration in the bar and packets of mini chocolate eggs were handed out to customers. He said a small pile of eggs were on the bar in front of him when he suddenly felt something hit the back of his chair. He found one of the eggs on the floor behind the chair, although no one had touched them.

Ellie has some beautiful 1940s Christmas decorations and they are normally kept in the cellar. On this same occasion several of these decorations 'appeared' on the floor in the bar. Ellie explained that some of them are really delicate and if they had been thrown they would have broken. There seemed to be no reason why they had appeared in the bar and the only explanation is that the spirit children joined in the celebration fun.

Ghosts Amongst the Fabric

Quality Textiles, the curtain and household linen shop in Surrey Street, once held the title of being the most haunted building in Littlehampton, but after Derek Acorah visited the shop in 2006 to film for a television series, he released some of the ghosts grounded in the building and it lost its title to the Dolphin Hotel. At the time, Derek Acorah told the owner, Ivor Holland, that he is a born medium and this was the reason why he could see and hear ghost spirits. Ivor thought no more about it until a business colleague Anthony Kesner, who taught at the College of Psychic Studies in London, persuaded him to join a course so that he could improve his skills and help him communicate with the ghosts that were now left in the building. His life has completely changed as he is now a fully fledged medium who is able to detect ghosts and talk to them.

Ivor and his wife Yvonne moved into No. 17 Surrey Street in the 1980s and within a week he began to hear footsteps upstairs and chairs being scraped across the floor. At first they thought someone had broken in, then after about three months they accepted the fact that their new shop was also home to several ghosts and instead of feeling scared, they felt protected. Ivor also had a very strange experience. Each time he went to look for stock he would say what he was looking for to remind himself of what he needed and, as if by magic, he would find the particular roll of curtaining he wanted slightly protruding or raised from the rest, so he could locate it easily. After a while he used this to his advantage and as he entered the stockroom would say out loud what he was looking for!

The couple decided to do some research and discovered that the building was constructed around 1740 and was much larger than the narrow shop it is today. One of the ghosts that can still be seen in the shop is the spirit of a tailor called William Dyer, who was known to the royal family as he worked for them when they stayed at the Pavilion in Brighton, and was therefore allowed to have the royal crest above the door. According to Ivor, William received a visit from Queen Victoria when she was staying at nearby Arundel Castle as she needed repairs to her cape after tearing it on a gorse bush while out riding. When I researched this story I discovered that William had been born in 1801 and was christened at St Mary's in Littlehampton. He appears in the 1841 census as a tailor and is listed on the 1871 census as still living in Surrey Street as a sixty-nine-year-old retired draper, having retired in 1865.

However, when Derek Acorah visited in 2006 he discovered that the main spirit in the building was that of a man called Charles. Interestingly, while Ivor and Yvonne were preparing for Derek's visit Ivor had a strange experience. He was perfectly happy about receiving Derek and the film crew and he had gone to the door to check if they had arrived when he had a strange feeling of not wanting Derek in the shop. Charles used to channel his energy through Ivor and this particularl night he felt as though Charles had his hand inside his body pulling on his spine. Derek confirmed this and informed Ivor that the reason Charles was grounded was because he loved the building and did not want to cross over to the other side for fear of not knowing what would greet him. In fact, Ivor has discovered that Charles didn't realise he had passed over and thought he was still alive and that Ivor was the ghost messing around with his stock! Little wonder Charles was upset.

Charles was a very precise man who, it seems, liked things it be in their place but also had a rather irritating and mischievous sense of humour. Above the door to the shop was a motion sensor which was connected to a buzzer, so that if Ivor and Yvonne were busy in the back of the building they would know if a customer had entered. If they were busy bringing stock down from upstairs they would always lock the door until the stock was in place. Every time Ivor did this he would only get as far as the third step on the stair and the buzzer would sound. He would rush back and find the door still locked and the shop empty. After a while Ivor got annoyed with Charles and told him to stop his fun, which he did. It is believed that when Charles was alive he had a small office upstairs close to the toilet, because every time after putting stock in this room Ivor would come into the shop in the morning to find stock thrown all over the floor. He explained to me that in the days when Charles owned the shop he would need to enter all the stock in a ledger by hand with a quill pen, so naturally when Ivor introduced new stock into the room, Charles was annoyed at having the task of recording everything. One afternoon a pillow was thrown, so Ivor told Charles off and immediately six more pillows came flying down from the shelf.

When Derek came to the shop he told Ivor that he could not set Charles free, but he gave Ivor some advice to help set the spirit free by telling him that he had seen his wife in the shop and it was best to let him go to her. Charles has been back to the shop on a number of occasions since, says Ivor, but he is usually seen in the corridor on the first floor, peering out of his office, near the toilet. On my visit to the shop I certainly felt an icy cold spot in the corridor and Ivor explained that this is where the spirits enter the shop. Charles is usually seen as the head and shoulders of a black silhouette peering out of his office, with his hands on the doorway, although at other times he is a shadowy figure. At the end of this corridor is a toilet, and one day the Hollands were entertaining a friend to tea. She asked if she could use the toilet, and minutes later Ivor heard a scream and rushed up the stairs. On investigating he learned that Charles had decided to make an appearance by peering out from the small office just as the woman was leaving the toilet, leaving her badly shaken.

In the back room on the ground floor resides the spirit of a little girl, Annabel, who is around eight years old and has long blonde hair. Annabel wears a pair of bright red shoes that were given to her by her grandfather, William Dyer. Annabel loved these shoes and wanted to wear them all day everyday, so they were kept at her grandfather's and she was only allowed to wear them on a Sunday to go to church. Annabel can often be heard skipping and dancing around in her shoes, and if you listen very carefully you may be lucky enough to hear her giggling in the shop. Ivor said she has a really hearty, infectious giggle. Annabel became grounded because she felt she was responsible for the death of her parents, who lived in one of the two thatched cottages next to the original building owned by William Dyer. They were burnt down and it is said candles that had been clipped to a tree around Christmas time caused the fire. Annabel thought that she had not blown them out properly one night before going to bed and was responsible for killing her parents. In fact, a piece of coal had fallen out of the fire and caused the disaster.

Mrs Holland told me how they eventually set Annabel free. One night they had a group of paranormal investigators to the house and Annabel went to sit on the lap of one of the investigators and said she was tired before snuggling up to him and going to sleep. Another of the team suggested that she should be set free. Suddenly Annabel's mother appeared and kissed one of Ivor's sons on the cheek then, although the room was in total darkness, a ball of light glowed from the corner of the room and they watched Annabel gently float away. Annabel still returns to the shop and Ivor told me that she is as solid as any human being.

Since becoming a medium Ivor has been able to find other ghosts in the building, including that of a sad young boy who was about six when he was purchased from the workhouse by the owner of the shop at that time. High in the back room is a cupboard with a narrow shelf which is locked with a very strong lock, too solid for such a small door. Ivor discovered from the spirit of the boy that he had to work at least twelve hours a day and as he suffered badly from asthma, he found this very difficult. If he did not do his work quickly enough, the owner would lock him in the cupboard for the night as punishment

Quality Textiles in Surrey Street, home to many ghosts.

The cupboard in Quality Textiles where the little boy was made to sleep. He still haunts the building.

and place a lighted candle on the shelf, which would have used up so much of the oxygen that it would have left the young boy struggling for air. He died when he was only eight years old.

Another spirit that resides in the loft space is that of a strange old man who for some unknown reason does not like women. If any woman tries to enter the loft he will push down on her head and leave her with a horrendous headache for days. Naturally when I was shown around the shop I didn't dare invade this gentleman's space. Yvonne tried to look in the loft one day and ended up with a headache that lasted for two days. It is believed that in life the old man was mentally disturbed, and as long as he is left alone he is harmless.

Ivor says there are also the happy sounds of children laughing and racing around as they play, and he says these are some of the same children that have been heard in the Dolphin Hotel. Ivor thinks that they once played with the children who lived in his shop.

The most recent spirit Ivor has been able to detect is that of an eighteen-year-old youth who he had mentored. Darryl had been badly abused as a child and had got into trouble with drugs. Ivor was a volunteer for the local services and had helped Darryl to get back on the right track, but just as he was getting his life together he was found dead after a heroin overdose, which Ivor thought was most strange. Darryl had dabbled in many drugs, but never touched heroin as he was frightened of needles. At the time of his death, Darryl was informing the police of local drug dealers so perhaps his death was not an overdose after all. For a while Darryl lived rough and as a consequence had really smelly feet. Yvonne says she can always tell when Darryl is in the shop because there is a dreadful smell.

The Hungry, Boozy Ghost

Further along Surrey Street from Quality Textiles is an off-licence called The Offie, which over the years has also been the scene of a lot of paranormal activity. The locks were changed by a previous manager because he believed that someone was breaking into the building at night and causing a disturbance. Cans of drink have been thrown onto the floor,

The Offie, Surrey Street.

while on one occasion staff arrived at the premises to discover that the fridge door had been left open. The staff have also reported someone walking around upstairs, and many will not enter the cellar because they feel that someone is watching them. The building was once a public house, frequented by sailors, and rumour informs us that a murder took place on the site after it was discovered that the wife of the landlord was having an affair. This may account for the activity of this angry ghost.

One Less Ghost!

On 20 April 2006, the *Littlehampton Gazette* reported that the Horror Hotel at Littlehampton Harbour Park had lost one of its ghosts, and revealed a grisly past. The hotel, a walk-through ghost train, was believed to have been the home to the ghost of a man who was murdered on the site just after the turn of the nineteenth century. One of the staff who had worked at the Park for seventeen years said she had seen the ghost several times, and there was the occasional odd chill about the place. She said the apparition had a great big hole in his stomach.

Derek Acorah, on a visit for his television programme, revealed that the man had died of a severe stomach injury after he was attacked by two men who had impaled him on a sharp weapon. Derek claimed that he had moved the ghost to the next realm and staff said that the weird atmosphere has now gone. The spirit had nothing to do with the fact that the building is called the Horror Hotel, but rather because of what had happened on the site in the past. Today the refurbished building includes the House of Mystery, but no strange encounters have taken place.

The House of Mystery at Littlehampton. This was the site of a murder between 1805 and 1810, and where Derek Acorah released the man's ghost.

Poling

Poling is a small village with Grade I and II listed buildings and is situated on the road to the south of the A27, about eight miles from Worthing. The Church of St Nicholas, which can only be reached by paths and stiles, has two interesting memorials; one is to Colin Cowdrey, the cricket legend, and there is also a rare plaque to the memory of Sir Harry Johnston, the explorer, naturalist, author and painter who died in 1927. This plaque was designed by Eric Gill, the Arts and Craft sculptor and typeface designer, in 1925, but was not released until 1929. It uses the typeface Perpetua.

At one time the author A.A. Milne and his son Christopher Robin lived in the seventeenth-century house at the eastern end of Poling. A swan on the lake by the house was named Hopper by Milne, and it was featured in one of the *Winnie the Pooh* books.

Monks Chanting at a Funeral

However, the village is also known for the well-documented story of ghostly chanting relating to the monks of Poling, who ran a minor house or preceptory of the Knights Templar. Interestingly, the chanting is accompanied by organ music even though this period is long before the organ was invented.

According to various reports, Martha Bates, who was born in 1870, was introduced to the fascinating world of ghosts by her grandfather and later she kept a journal of her supernatural experiences. Having heard stories about the monks of Poling she asked the owner of St John's Priory if she could visit with a relative. They duly arrived and spent six long nights at the house, but did not hear a sound. On the last night they were sitting huddled together with blankets to try and keep warm in a draughty corridor when they suddenly heard chanting. It started off in the distance before growing louder and louder as though a procession of monks was walking past them, then the chanting faded and finally trailed off. Her relative, who was a professor of music, immediately recognised the music as a Gregorian funeral chant.

Over the years the priory has been added to and only a small part of the original thirteenth-century chapel can be seen. Later it was used by the Knights Hospitallers of St John of Jerusalem and was more recently owned by Sir Harry Johnston, who carried out many improvements to the building. His brother Philip heard the Gregorian chants on several occasions when he visited and when he realised that the chant was always the same, wrote down the notes. He sent the score to a friend who was an expert on ancient music and he recognised it a Gregorian setting of the 'Deus Misereatur', the 67th Psalm, which is used at funerals.

Arundel

Arundel began life as a Saxon village and it has been suggested that the name derives from a corruption of Saxon words *harune dell* meaning 'horehound (a type of plant) valley'. In 1067 the castle was built, and by the next year Arundel had become a flourishing market town. Arundel Castle came to be owned by the Fitzalan family, and by the sixteenth century it passed to the Dukes of Norfolk, by which time Arundel had become a busy port with ships sailing from the town along the River Arun to the sea, five miles away.

A Castle with a Host of Ghosts

Ten miles from Worthing, in the town of Arundel, sits the magnificent Arundel Castle. It was founded on Christmas Day 1067 after William the Conqueror successfully invaded England and claimed the throne. One-third of Sussex, as well as lands in the Welsh Marches, was granted by William I to Roger de Montgomery, a cousin of William's, as a reward for remaining in Normandy to keep law and order whilst William was busy in England. When Roger de Montgomery died the castle reverted to the Crown under Henry I, who in turn willed it and the surrounding land to his second wife, Adeliza of Louvain. Three years after Henry died she married William d'Albini II, the 1st Earl of the d'Aubigny family of Saint-Martin-d'Aubigny in Normandy. Since 1138 Arundel Castle and the earldom, except for it occasionally being returned to the Crown, have passed through the generations as the seat of the Dukes of Norfolk. The 16th Duke had planned to give the castle to the National Trust but the 17th Duke instead created an independent charitable trust to protect the castle, which is currently in the hands of the 18th Duke and remains the principle family home. The castle was severely damaged by fire in the seventeenth century but has been restored to its former glory. In 1846 Queen Victoria and her husband Prince Albert visited Arundel Castle and were entertained by Henry Charles, 13th Duke of Norfolk. Could this have been when she had her cape repaired by William Dyer at Littlehampton?

Arundel Castle is the home of several ghosts and some claim there are at least seven. The saddest of all must be the spirit of a small boy who is thought to have worked in the kitchens around 200 years ago. It is believed that his master used to beat him, and one day he hurt him so badly that the poor boy died. His ghost has never been seen, but has been heard on many occasions scurrying around the kitchen or feverishly scrubbing the pots and pans.

An apparition of a man has been seen in the library wearing clothing of the Charles II period and has now become known as the 'Blue Man' because he is dressed in blue silk garments. He has been seen by custodians and appears to be searching through or reading the books, although it is never the same book, and he only stays for a minute or two before disappearing. He has been seen since 1630, so perhaps he is searching for some lost fact, an inventory or a will? The library is also haunted by a little black dog that is said to have belonged to St Philip Howard, 13th Earl of Arundel, during the reign of Elizabeth I. The earl was sentenced to death for failing to renounce the Roman Catholic faith, although the sentence was never carried out and he instead spent eleven years in the Tower of London accompanied by his dog. He died in 1595 and was canonised by Pope Paul VI in 1970 as one of the Forty Martyrs of England and Wales. Several of the guides at the castle have been asked, always by children, who the little dog in the library is. As yet, no adult has ever reported seeing the dog.

Arundel Castle, which has a long history and several ghosts.

Hiorne Tower. Look out for the lady dressed in white searching for her lover.

An unusual ghost is that of a small white bird seen fluttering around the windows of the castle on many occasions. The timing of these appearances would appear to indicate the imminent death of someone connected to the castle and has included the death of Henry, 15th Duke of Norfolk, in 1917.

The ghost of a young lady dressed in white can be seen at Hiorne Tower in Arundel Park, which is within the grounds of the castle. It is an excellent example of a folly, noted for its odd triangular construction, and was built in the late eighteenth century by the architect Francis Hiorne to demonstrate his skills to the Duke of Norfolk. Legend informs us that she killed herself by jumping off the tower when rejected by her lover. She can be seen from the top of the tower looking for him.

The most recent sighting of a ghost was by a trainee footman in 1958. It was his duty to switch off the drawbridge lights in the evening, and on this particular night he was halfway along the drawbridge when he was aware of someone about 15ft in front of him going in the same direction. As he got nearer to the person he could see the head and shoulders of a man, who was wearing a light grey tunic with loose sleeves. He had longish hair and he guessed he was in his early twenties. The footmen said the image was like an old photograph with the outline blurred, and he could see nothing below waist level. As he walked on the apparition seemed to fade and then disappeared completely. The terrified footman ran back along the drawbridge and forgot to switch off the lights.

The Leaping Ghost and Ringing Telephones

The Norfolk Arms hotel in the High Street was built around 1783 and has been extended. It was badly damaged by a fire in 1937 and during the Second World War became the home of Canadian troops. It has also been the scene of paranormal activities. In the 1980s there were reports of the radio being switched on and off in the kitchen by an unseen hand, while saucepans and pots would fly off the shelves for no apparent reason.

One day Hazel Sampson, who was working at the hotel at the time, saw the figure of a man who was stripped to the waist who proceeded to leap from the window into the back yard. She told the *Worthing Herald* at the time that she found this most odd as the window had not been fitted until the 1950s, so she assumed that the ghost must have been related to some more recent incident. Although this incident was left unresolved, according to local rumour one of the hotel bedrooms was the scene of a murder in the 1800s, so perhaps the spirit is of the murderer trying to make his escape.

A recent sinister experience took place in 1992 when the telephone rang in Room 10. When the occupants of the room picked up the receiver there was no one on the line, so they rang down to reception but were told that no one had rung Room 10. Later reception received a call from Room 10 but, again, no one answered. When reception rang the room they were told by the occupants that they had not made a call. Was this simply a fault on the line or something more sinister?

The Norfolk Arms, where there have been reports of a leaping ghost and ringing telephones.

A sign for a spooky trip to Arundel Jail.

Further up the road on the left-hand side is the Town Hall and jail, built in 1836 by the 12th Duke of Norfolk. It was used until 2002 as the cells for those appearing in the court at Arundel, which was then situated above the jail. Now it is used as a spooky tourist attraction which claims to have many spirits behind its doors, including a Grey Lady, an armless man, a priest and a youth who allegedly stabbed himself to avoid being executed.

Nuns, a Priest and an Eerie Atmosphere

It is not known when the first Church of St Nicholas, the parish and priory church of Arundel, was built, but the Domesday survey records that a church dedicated to St Nicholas existed between the years 1042 and 1066 and would probably have been rebuilt sometime in the Norman period. The church is unusual because it is the home of two denominations, Roman Catholic and the Church of England. In 1836 the Fitzalan Chapel was relinquished by the Corporation in exchange for land on which to build the new Town Hall. In 1874 a brick wall was built next to the grille to divide the church, which resulted in a legal argument involving the Roman Catholic Duke of Norfolk and the then Church of England rector, Revd G. Arbuthnot, and a group of nuns who had been allowed to use the Fitzalan Chapel. However, in 1879 the High Court ruled that the chapel belonged to the Duke of Norfolk and the unique situation of two churches of different denominations sharing the same church was created. The late Bernard Marmaduke, 16th Duke of Norfolk, who was a leading Roman Catholic layman, did a lot to break down the barriers that existed and as an ecumenical gesture had the upper part of the wall taken down in 1956. The lower half was removed in 1968 and the Fitzalan Chapel is now separated by a grille and a glass screen and can only be accessed via the castle.

In 1983 the Wilkinson family visited the castle with their children, and while the parents visited the chapel the children played happily on the grassy bank outside. Mrs Wilkinson suddenly felt strangely drawn to one of the female effigies depicted in Elizabethan costume on the tomb in one of the side aisles. She turned to tell her husband but he felt so icy cold and had such a strong feeling of resentment from the tomb that he had decided to leave the chapel. Interestingly two friends of the family visited the chapel a few years later and, without knowing of their friends' previous experience, also reported a cold chill and a feeling of aggressive hostility in the same spot.

During the English Civil War the Roundheads used the Fitzalan Chapel as a barracks and the soldiers smashed all the stained glass and mutilated the effigies. The chapel was also used to stable the horses amongst the marble figures of the earls and dukes, and some say that this accounts for the eerie, icy chill that has been experienced by visitors to the church.

On 31 January 1975, Bernard Marmaduke died and not long after the funeral one of the churchwardens, Howard Frith, happened to look into the chapel from St Nicholas' side and noticed who he assumed to be a white-haired family mourner kneeling before the altar. The woman was dressed in a long blue robe and it was not until he mentioned her to the gardener that he realised that he had seen a ghost! The gardener informed him that the chapel was locked and he had the key in his pocket. Both men went to check and found that the door was still locked and no one was inside.

The most unusual incident occurred back in the 1940s when a well-respected solicitor took a photograph of the interior of the church, and on receiving the prints was astonished to see 'a shadowy robed figure', possibly that of a priest, standing in front of the altar. He was puzzled because at the time he took the photograph he was the only person in the church. There have also been reports of a figure of a nun in a grey habit that has been seen by the town crier, whose duty it was to visit the church each evening to wind up the clock. Each time she was seen sitting on a chair but within a few moments would

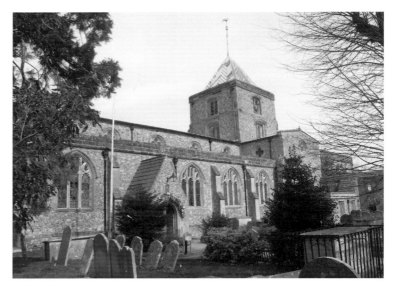

*The Church of
St Nicholas.*

*Fitzalan Chapel has a
strange atmosphere.*

vanish, chair and all! Almost a year later the town crier saw the same nun on the stairway of the bell tower. Several years passed before visitors to the church also reported seeing an apparition of a woman in the bell tower. Behind the landing where she was seen was an oak door, leading onto a wooden platform, and it was thought that during the Civil War this was used as a lookout point. The nun is suspected to have been one of the nuns from the nearby convent of the Poor Clares who may have jumped or fallen from this platform.

One of the most recent hauntings occurred in December 1995 when a bell-ringer was going up the stairs and found that he was following an unknown person, who had promptly disappeared by the time he had reached the bell chamber.

3

East of Worthing

Sompting

The village of Sompting is located between Lancing and Worthing at the foot of the South Downs. The unusual name of Sompting, which was originally known as Sultinges, is mentioned in the Domesday survey of 1086 as being in the Hundred of Brightford. The name is thought to derive from the Old English for 'dwellers by the marsh'. The south Saxons settled in this part of Sussex around AD 550 and most probably built a small, timber-framed church where the tower stands today, occupying a rather isolated position, because since 1939 the church has been separated from the village by the busy A27.

Church Protected by the Knights Templar?

The Anglo-Saxon Church of St Mary the Virgin is a Grade I listed building which was added to by the Templars and is the oldest and most extraordinary church associated with this ancient order. The unusual tower standing 80ft high is an early example of a 'Rhenish Helm', a four-sided, gabled pyramidal cap which is unique England. It is thought that it was built in stages and constructed from flint bonded with lime mortar, measuring 3ft thick. The church was adapted by the Normans in 1154 when William de Braose granted it to the Order of the Temple of Solomon in Jerusalem, a crusading order of fighting monks known as the Templars. In 1324, under the international ruling of the Pope, all Templar properties were assigned to another order of crusaders, the order of the Hospital of St John of Jerusalem, known as the Knights of St John or the Hospitallers. Graves of some Knights Templar have been found in the grounds of the church. The Hospitallers' chapel attached to the north wing of the church continues today in its original role as a chapel for the St John's Ambulance.

Whilst there are no official reports of ghosts in the vicinity, people have reported seeing what they described as a dark shadow flitting from tree to tree which has followed them as they approach the church from the A27. As with many churches and grounds associated with the Knights Templar, it is said that they guard their properties in death as they did in life. Some mediums have reported seeing shadowy figures standing at the four corners of the church watching that no trouble is caused to their departed comrades.

In August 2004 a group from COTC (Children of the City) Paranormal Investigations and the WSPI (West Sussex Paranormal Investigations) visited the church and churchyard. One of the group reported what he could only describe as a dark figure standing next to a bush. Was this a trick of the light or did he really see a ghostly figure? As they headed towards the church via the graveyard, another of the party saw lights on the ground. At first they thought it may be torch lights but these lights were different, more like pinpricks of light than beams from a torch. As they approached a grave another in the group got a strange feeling, as though the grave was giving off energy, and as he got closer the energy got much stronger. They read the gravestone and established that he had no links with the woman buried there, so why was he feeling this strange power?

They then decided to move towards the church and one of the party, whom I shall refer to by the initial C., saw a head bobbing along the other side of the stone wall. They checked where everyone was at the time and discovered that no one was near where C. had seen the head. One of the women in the group walked to the trees near the car park claiming it was a hanging tree. Whilst the group stood looking at it, C. saw a figure and from the description it matched perfectly with the figure that another member of the group had seen standing next to a bush earlier in the night.

The group found a suitable spot to hold a séance near the church, and linked hands. The name 'Jack' was mentioned and it was not until later that they discovered that C.'s grandfather was known as Jack. One started to channel a spirit who sounded very scared,

Sompting Church, a Templar church that may still be guarded by the Knights.

and they felt it was crying, and the words, 'he's coming' and then the word 'murder' were uttered. As this was taking place C. felt it was the spirit of a young girl and all agreed that it was definitely a female spirit. Could it have been someone who had been murdered and buried at St Mary's still being haunted by her killer? C. started to see the spirit lights again in the direction of the grave that had made him feel so strange earlier on, and a closer look at the grave revealed that it was the grave of a lady who had died in 2000 and fresh flowers had been placed on the grave. Could it have been the anniversary of her death that was causing all the energy? A fuller report of this investigation, written by Arron Weedall, can be found on www.wspi.co.uk

One evening two Worthing ladies, Joyce Elsden and Jean Robertson, together with another lady, Peggy Green from Surrey, were travelling along the road that leads from Sompting Church to Sompting Abbots School. They noticed about twenty lit candles spread across the road forming the unique shape of a Maltese cross, a symbol used by the Knights Templar. It was drizzling and what struck the ladies was that despite the rain the candles remained alight. Puzzled, they stopped the car to take a closer look but did not get out because at that point another car travelling behind overtook them and drove past as though nothing unusual was happening. When the three ladies, who coincidentally were travelling home after attending a talk on the Knights Templar, looked again, the candles had gone. They drove on and Jean, who was sitting in the back of car, says that at the time it did not occur to her to turn around and look out of the back window to see if the candles were still there, something she regrets to this day. All three ladies are convinced that they had seen the candles and not imagined them. The following morning Jean was driving past the exact same spot and decided to stop the car and take a closer look of the road, and to her utter amazement discovered that there were bits of melted candle wax still on the road. Were the Knights Templar who are reputed to guard this church trying to communicate to these ladies who had listened to talk about them, or were they trying to assure them that they were still present in this world? We must draw our own conclusions.

The Hospitallers' Chapel, now used as a chapel by St John's Ambulance.

Shoreham-on-Sea

This delightful little seaside town was established by the Normans in the late eleventh century and is mentioned in the Doomsday survey. It became a seaport and the future King Charles II hid in the town during the English Civil War before he escaped to the Continent. It had its own busy shipyards in Victorian times and has a long history relating to smuggling and contraband, but it was also one of the principal ports that launched the D-Day invasion of Normandy in June 1944. The town is also well known for being described by ghost-tour operators as 'spooky Shoreham'.

Strange Wailing from the Cemetery

Some of the older residents who lived in Shoreham during the 1940s can recall hearing a haunting wailing coming from Mill Lane cemetery that was enough to send anyone passing through the cemetery late at night to run for the safety of the bright lights and the main road. It is thought that these piercing cries were the weeping of the dearly departed who were buried in the graves, but others insist that it is the spirit of the mariners lost at sea who had not been buried in their home towns as they wished. A walk around the cemetery will reveal many interesting and ornate graves of sea farers.

Mill Lane Cemetery. Are the mariners in this cemetery moaning because they wish to be buried in their home towns?

Ringing Bells and a Man in Green Overalls

The modern red-brick building of Adur Civic Centre at Ham Road does not seem the right place for ghostly activities, but research into the history of the site may help to explain a little. The building is partly built on the site of the Coliseum, a theatre constructed to entertain the troops who were training at Shoreham during the First World War, and partly on the site of St Aubryn's Street and Albion cottages. Strange cold spots and doors swinging open on their own have been reported, but the most unusual activity concerns the ship's bell from the sloop HMS *Shoreham* which hangs in the reception area about 10ft above the ground. On various occasions, usually around 6 p.m. or 7 p.m., a single chime has been heard from this bell, despite there being no sign of movement from the rope or the clapper. During an event at the Civic Centre in 1996 there were loud peals from the bell, but people sitting directly under it said they saw no one pulling the short length of rope which is well beyond of the reach of a person of normal height.

In the autumn of the same year a presenter on Coastway Hospital Radio, Ben Chapman, was alone in the building when he heard a series of muted taps on the bell. More recently an apparition has been seen moving rapidly towards the coffee machine on the first floor. The unknown ghost has been nicknamed Charlie by the cleaning staff and is fully accepted as being friendly, but no connection has been found to the bell-ringing exploits. Staff of Coastway Hospital Radio, who have seen the figure when leaving their tiny studio, claim that the green-clad figure disappears just before reaching the end of the corridor. One feasible explanation for the ghost is that it is the former caretaker of the Coliseum, by now a cinema, who was accidentally electrocuted. A Shoreham resident recalls that the cinema later became a factory producing hydraulic pumps and that one evening an odd-job man came running down the stairs from the canteen shouting that he had just seen a ghost. Perhaps this was an apparition of Charlie?

Adur Civil Centre. Who is Charlie and why does the ship's bell ring?

Lady in Grey

The medical records section of Southlands Hospital dates from the 1970s and is located in the basement, directly beneath the out patients' department adjacent to Hammy Lane. It is claimed to have been haunted by a Grey Lady and it is reported that during the 1980s staff and porters did not like going to the medical section out of hours in fear of bumping into the ghost. Prior to the hospital being built there was a house at this location and as ghosts tend to haunt sites and don't just disappear because a new building is erected, the haunting may date from that time with the Grey Lady being disturbed whilst building went on. Who is she and why does she haunt the site?

Ghosts of Children

The site of Somerfields in Shoreham was in the past occupied by a school and a workhouse before the building was finally demolished in 1979 for the erection of the supermarket. Apparitions of young girls smartly dressed in grey dresses and white pinafores have been seen on the site, together with a phantom man in black with a top hat. It is thought these were the former occupants of the workhouse and that the man in black is in charge. Another possible explanation could be that these were the pupils from the time the school stood on the site and the man is the headmaster. Why do these children still haunt the site?

The site of the old workhouse in Shoreham. Why do children still haunt this site?

An Old Man and Happy Laughing Children

The Crown and Anchor in the High Street, Shoreham-on-Sea, is guarded by a giant effigy of a swashbuckling buccaneer, a fitting reminder of this seaside town's smuggling past. In the eighteenth century it was known as Amplefords and over the years the building has gone through many changes which have taken away some of its character. Its origin probably goes back to at least the seventeenth century and part of the staircase that can be seen in the bar dates to around 1700. The magnificent pirate outside the pub seen clutching a crown was carved in the 1930s from a single block of teak to replace an earlier figurehead which a previous landlord had brought with him from the Royal George, a pub further down the street.

Over the years there have been several sightings of ghosts on the site, which is thought to have once been the location of a hanging. One night the son of a previous landlord suddenly woke from his sleep to see a pair of legs dangling above him. It transpired that the night before there had been a séance and this could well have evoked the apparition of a hanged man. It is also claimed that the ghost of a Spaniard haunts the pub, but it is not clear if this is the same ghost as the hanged man, but it is said that there are smugglers' tunnels running beneath the pub.

The present owner, Giles Stone, who has run the pub for four years, said he has heard nothing about the ghosts mentioned above but has had a few unusual experiences himself.

The Crown and Anchor public house. Do seafarers still frequent this pub?

At the end of the evening he makes sure that all the lights are off and checks the alarm is set, but on more than one occasion he has found the alarm turned off and then back on again. In the bar area he has also caught a glimpse of an old man with a beard sitting in the corner, perfectly harmlessly appearing to finish his drink, but when Giles turned around again the man had vanished. Perhaps it is the spirit of an old fisherman enjoying a pint at his local, but whoever he is he is content to sit quietly and not interfere with the customers or running of the public house.

The manageress, who has worked in the pub for around six years, said it is her job to check on the back of the pub, which is split between two levels. She often sees the ghostly figures of two children playing happily in the area between the two bars. She also checks that the audio system is switched off and unplugged, but on several occasions, despite the system being unplugged, she has heard music and talking as though the radio is still on. She has listened carefully to try and make out what is being said but it appears to be in a language she does recognise. Is it a group of seafaring fishermen chatting amongst themselves in a broad Sussex dialect that she hears? Whatever spirits choose to frequent this delightful pub that fronts onto the High Street, and has an excellent view onto the mouth of the River Adur from the back, they are certainly happy, friendly beings and seem content to remain in their world.

Moving barrels for fun!

Until the 1990s the Ferry Inn at No. 1 East Street had a mischievous ghost who obviously wanted to be the centre of attention. Puzzled staff would find that casks of beer and barrels had been moved around the cellar for no apparent reason, but it is known that the Ferry Inn used to be connected by tunnels to the Waterside Inn on the opposite side of the river bank and no doubt was the haunt of many a smuggler. The present owner, Mike Chapman, took over the pub sixteen years ago and since then it appears that the ghost has vanished completely, leaving Mike and his customers to enjoy their surroundings.

Above: *The Ferry Inn. Who used to move the barrels?*

Right: *A plaque outside the Ferry Inn, a reminder of when there was a ferry service across the River Adur to the opposite side.*

Spooky Cellars

The Waterside inn in Ferry Road on the opposite side of the river bank has a picturesque view of the River Adur and it is hard to believe that this idyllic-looking inn has reported some strange events over the years. The inn was previously called the Lady Jane and is built on a site once occupied by a Carmelite nunnery, which may account for the many reported apparitions of nuns and monks witnessed by past owners. Former licensees Julie and Dean Lawton were interviewed by Janet Cameron for her book *Paranormal Brighton and Hove* and they told her that although they had not actually seen any apparitions themselves, they did have some spooky tales to tell. In the middle of the night they would hear chairs being scraped and moved about, although they knew that no one else was in the pub at the time.

A number of tunnels run from the pub and although the small, square entrances are blocked up and are set a few feet above ground, they are still visible today. Two of the tunnels once went under the river to the Ferry Inn on the other side of the bank. The long tunnels are now backfilled and the huge cellars below the inn could be the source of the strange happenings. The Lawtons had their office in the cellar and grew to live with their spooky guests. They told Janet that normally the cellar was very warm to work in, but on a number of occasions the temperature dropped to icy cold, and although it only lasted for around ten to fifteen seconds, the cold atmosphere appeared to come from nowhere and sent shivers done the spine. Frequently beer being served in the bar would go flat for

The Waterside on the opposite side of the river.

Above: *Stairs to the cellars at the Waterside. The previous landlord's dogs would not go down these stairs.*

Above right: *The landlord revealing another tunnel at the Waterside Inn.*

Right: *Another tunnel at the Waterside.*

no apparent reason and when they went down into the cellar to investigate, they would find that the gas had been turned off. Staff were adamant they had not turned off the gas as due to health and safety reasons they were not allowed into the cellars. Apparently this happened at least nine times.

Two dogs belonging to the landlord were well used to running up and down the stairs in the pub but would not venture down to the cellar, sensing something was not right below. However, in 2008 the adventurous poltergeist, obvious bored with the cellar, decided to explore upstairs. The landlady's father was in the living room with the couple's white German shepherd dog and had just put a picture on the wall. He was standing back to see if it was straight when suddenly the dog backed away and started to growl. Its hackles rose and sudden the dog went 'mad'. Animals are more sensitive than humans and can often sense things that are not visible to us. One wonders if the ghost retreated back to the cellar for good or will he venture upstairs again?

Did Little Rose and her Nanny Drown?

The Suter's Yard in the High Street has been known by a number of names; in past years it has been called the Schooner, the High Street Bar, the Ship and the Wood on the Nose. It is said that the ghost of a little red-haired girl had been seen sitting on the floor in front of the bar and in the lobby to the ladies' toilets. Shortly after moving into the Schooner in August 1990 the landlady noticed a female figure in the cellar and her husband could also sense the presence strongly. Meanwhile, their eight-year-old daughter was always talking about a little girl. 'Who's your little friend?' enquired her curious parents. 'The little girl who lives the cellar,' said the child. In fact, there were so many strange happenings during that first month that the couple decided to seek the help of spiritualists.

Suter's Yard. Is this where Rose was drowned?

One Saturday they gathered together in the pub to see what could be done to help. Suddenly one of them collapsed on the floor and began to speak in a childish voice. A story unfolded and it appears that these were the spirits of two people, one an eight-year-old girl, exactly the same age as the couple's child, and the girl's nanny, who was twenty-six. Apparently they had both drowned in the cellar when there was a sudden flood. The young nanny kept repeating that she wanted to go home so an exorcism was recommended, but it is not known if this took place as the strange happenings continued.

By 1995 there were new people running the pub, but they only stayed for eight months. During that time Philip, one of the managers, saw the little red-haired girl sitting on the floor by the front door of the bar. He watched, puzzled and astonished, until the girl gradually faded away in front of his eyes. He also reported seeing the figure of a woman in black standing some distance from the bar. She was similarly seen by Jordan, the young son of the next managers, the Hamiltons, and he started having long conversations with the little girl, called Rose, and could not understand why his parents could not see her too.

There have also been reports of a child giggling and of a large orb (described variously as blue or white) that floated above the head of the little red-haired girl. It is also understood that the cellar in the pub was once used as the town's mortuary, where the bodies of drowned fishermen were kept prior to burial. Footsteps have also been heard when no one is around. Lorna Parker, who took over the pub in 2006, said she was aware of the ghost stories but she personally had not seen any ghosts. Today the pub has yet another new manager who told me he had seen nothing, so perhaps the ghosts have finally found a resting place; only time will tell.

4

North of Worthing

Steyning

There is no mention of Steyning before the Saxon period, although we do know that Bronze Age man travelled the ancient trackways around this area and had a settlement on Round Hill, just above Steyning. Not every town can say that it has its own saintly legend, but Steyning is first mentioned in a legend concerning St Cuthman, who founded a wooden church in the town during the late eighth or ninth century. Visitors may wonder at the town signs; one shows a sturdy peasant lad pushing a woman along in a four-wheeled wooden chair, while the other is of her in a wheelbarrow-like conveyance.

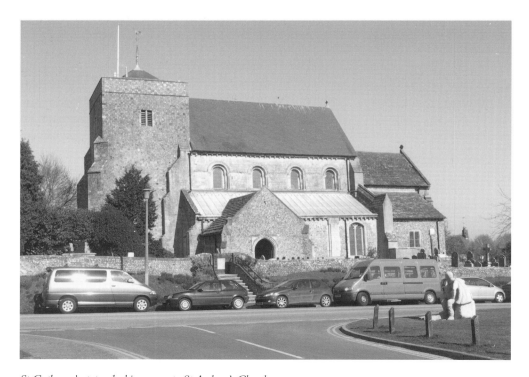

St Cuthman's statue, looking across to St Andrew's Church.

A closer view of St Cuthman, with the wheelbarrow in which he transported his mother.

Legend informs us that St Cuthman was born in AD 681, probably in Devon or Cornwall. He was a poor shepherd whose widowed mother was paralysed, so whenever he travelled he pushed his mother in a wheelbarrow with a rope placed around his shoulders to help support the weight. By the time he came to a field in Steyning he was very tired and when the rope snapped, he decided this was a sign from God to build a church, which is now called St Andrew's. Apparently St Cuthman had trouble fixing a roof beam in place and a stranger appeared and showed him how to do it. When St Cuthman asked the stranger his name, he was told, 'I am He in whose name you are building this church'. During his lifetime St Cuthman performed a number of spectacular miracles, and today a fine statue of him is overlooking the road to the church he founded. It is also interesting to note that the playwright Christopher Fry based *The Boy with a Cart* on the saint's early life and his coming to Steyning.

Moaning Milian

An article in the *Argus* on 13 February 2007 mentioned that Rupert Matthews, author of numerous paranormal and ghost books, claimed that the fine Church of St Andrews is haunted not by St Cuthman but Milian, a holy woman who arrived at the church in the thirteenth century looking for holiness and enlightenment. At first the local people were kind and welcoming, but it soon became apparent that the holy woman was argumentative, starting lawsuits against the local vicars and making herself an extremely unpopular lady. It is said that after her death, her ghost continued to appear to show the residents that she disapproved of the current priest. However, something must have pleased Milian because her presence began to fade and nowadays she is merely seen flitting around the churchyard. Is the statue of St Cuthman watching over the church he founded keeping Milian in order?

Bramber

Unlike Steyning, Bramber was more or less founded in the Norman period. The Battle Abbey chronicles show that Bramber did exist before the Domesday survey, but being a late development it did not appear in the book. The hill on which the ruined castle of Bramber sits must have been a prime site for early man, yet no evidence of habitation has been found pre-dating the Norman period. The name 'Bramber' is thought to mean a 'bramble thicket', although others claim it is an Old Saxon word *Brymmbuth* meaning 'a fortified place'. Bramber Castle was built around 1073 by William de Braose after the Battle of Hastings, replacing a Saxon one built about 100 years earlier to guard the then busy port on the River Adur. In its day it must have been very impressive, standing some 120ft above the river on a knoll. The castle, built of knapped flints and pebbles, became the centre of administration for the rape of Bramber with the living quarters and the storerooms situated at the base of the mound, which is still visible today.

William set about establishing his new Borough of Bramber as a port and built a bridge with a causeway to connect Bramber Castle with the port of Bramber. By 1086 he was charging a toll at his bridge on all ships passing to and from the port at Steyning, and the church below the castle served as a chapel for the residents of the castle.

Little is left of the castle today; the most noteworthy part remaining is a part of the 76ft-high keep wall, plus parts of the curtain wall, and a pre-Norman Conquest motte found within the walls.

There are a number of rather sad ghostly tales relating to the castle and in recent times English Heritage has banned ghost hunters from carrying out night time activities for fear of injury through potholes, tree roots and low branches. The ghostly history of Bramber comes from two recorded events: the first concerns the children of the 3rd William de Braose, who was involved in the events leading up to the Magna Carta being signed in 1215 and who disapproved of King John's actions; the second is the story of Lady Maud, who is still lamenting the death of her lover who was murdered by her husband.

Four Ragged Children Begging for Food

When William the Conqueror arrived in England he granted William de Braose no less than thirty-eight manors, as well as large estates in places as far afield as Dorset, Hampshire and Wales, but the principal home for the family was at Bramber Castle. The family became very powerful and when King John came to the throne he considered the family to be a threat to him, but it was the grandson of this dynasty who was to be the victim of King John's evil deeds.

William (1153-1211) had married Maud, known as Matilda de St Valery (1155-1210), and the couple had five children, although the heir, Reginald, was much older than his

Bramber Castle.

four siblings. Reginald went to live in a castle in Ireland, whilst the four younger children remained at Bramber with their parents. In Wales Maud was known as Moll Walbee and the locals people saw her as a supernatural being, having allegedly built Hay Castle in one night, carrying the stones in her apron.

Legend informs us that around 1208, William de Braose fell out of favour with the king, so King John sent a message to Bramber Castle informing the family that he wanted the children as hostages to ensure the family would remain loyal to the Crown. Maude hastily replied that she could not entrust her children to a monarch who had murdered his nephew, Prince Arthur, whom he had promised to protect. When the messenger returned without the children the king was furious and William, knowing that Bramber Castle would not withstand a siege, fled to Ireland with his family. They landed safely but Maud and the children were captured, taken back to London and then by barge to Windsor Castle, where they were thrown into the dungeons and left to starve to death. William de Braose eventually managed to escape to France via Shoreham, disguised 'in the habit of a beggar', but he was stripped of all his lands and died a year later in Corbeil, near Paris.

Some say his death was caused by a broken heart. It is said that gaunt ghosts of two, three or four of his children, depending on the writer, return to Bramber at Christmas time and can be seen begging in the village for bread or looking intently towards the ruined castle.

The Knight and His Lover

In the village of Bramber stands Lavender Cottage, and it was said sometime towards the end of the fifteenth century that Sir William de Lindfield dug a tunnel between the castle and the cottage of Sir Hubert de Hurst so that he could meet Sir Hubert's wife, Maud, with whom he had fallen in love. Each morning Sir William would come through the tunnel and meet Maud of Ditchling in the garden and this continued until Sir Hubert found out and decided to put an end to it once and for all by bricking up the tunnel. One morning as the knight came through the tunnel from Bramber Castle he realised that the tunnel had been blocked; when he turned back he found that the castle end of the tunnel had been blocked too. It is said that Maud searched for her lover and found him just as the last few bricks were being laid in place, walling him up alive. Being a cruel, jealous man, Sir Hubert would not let his wife near the tunnel, even though she could hear the terrible screams of her lover begging for food. Eventually Sir William died of starvation and it is said that Lady Maud killed herself so she could be reunited with her knight. Sir Hubert was so distraught when his wife died that he went mad and hanged himself in the cottage. The ghost of Sir Hubert is said to haunt the cottage, whilst the ghosts of the two lovers haunt the garden.

When the castle was attacked and occupied by the Parliamentarian troops during the Civil War, a skeleton of Sir William de Lindfield was discovered crouched in a corner, elbows on his knees and his head resting on his hands. Peter Underwood states in his book *This Haunted Isle: The Ghosts and Legends of Britain's Historic Buildings* that several Bramber residents reported hearing the sound of a woman wailing amongst the castle ruins, and they believed that what they were hearing were the sounds of Maud sobbing for her lover. Some also reported the sighting of a ghostly white horse that galloped around the now dried-up moat on moonlit nights. Could this have been Sir William's horse waiting for his master to return?

St Mary's, the Sele Priory Monks, the Little Elizabethan Girl and the White Lady

In the village of Bramber stands the magnificent timber-framed house of St Mary's which has featured in a number of television broadcasts, including the famous *Dr Who* series. It is a house that is brimming with mystery, legends and ghosts who live comfortably with its present owners. Sadly its full history may never be told as a number of its secrets have been taken to the grave with its past residents, but slowly its fascinating story is beginning to emerge. It is thanks to two extremely talented people who care passionately about its restoration and maintenance that we can now take a step back in time and enjoy what this splendid house has to offer. In 1984, Peter Thorogood, well-known author, composer, literary historian and leading authority on the nineteenth-century poet Thomas Hood (1799-1845), together with Roger Linton, a gifted designer, restorer and conservator, who trained at the Royal College of Art, combined their finances, talents and skills to purchase this medieval house from the brink of demolition and renovate it to its former glory.

Like many old houses, it has a number of ghosts, and to understand the mysterious hauntings associated with the house it is worth outlining its long and fascinating history.

The present building was refashioned in around 1470 by William of Waynflete, Bishop of Winchester and founder of Magdalen College, Oxford. It was built as an inn for pilgrims who needed to rest on their way to pay homage at the tomb of St Thomas of Canterbury, but its origins go back much further, to the days of the Knights Templar. It all began when Philip de Braose, son of William de Braose, went out on the First Crusade in 1099 and entered Jerusalem opening up the Holy Land for pilgrims to visit. This led to the founding of the Order of Knights of the Temple of Jerusalem, and upon the death of Philip in 1125, his widow, Lady Aanor, bequeathed five acres of land at Bramber to the Knights Templar. The land was on a reclaimed promontory adjacent to the new causeway, which was used to build a Templar chapter house. It is interesting to note that some 900 years later, in 1990, during the renewal of the floor in the ground-floor rooms, an old hearth – possibly Templar – was discovered, together with a primitive plinth made of vertical clay tiles. The Knights stayed at Bramber until 1154 before moving to Sompting. Around 1190, the old timber bridge across the western channel was replaced by a splendid four-arched stone bridge with a chapel dedicated to St Mary the Virgin on the central pier. The bridge was eventually given to the Benedictine Priory of Sele by John de Braose in 1230, and fragments of the wooden bridge can be seen in the house today.

The chapter house, or Chapel House as it came to be called, passed to the monks of Sele, four of whom served as wardens of the bridge and ran the house as an inn, but

St Mary's at Bramber in 2009.

thanks to mismanagement by the monks, the future of the house was left in a precarious position; by all accounts the monks were rather prone to riotous behaviour. By 1320 the Chapel House and the bridge had fallen into decay, and had become so impoverished that they were excused from paying taxes. By 1459 the link between the priory at Sele and its parent abbey at Saumur had dissolved and the priory, along with its lands, came under the control of the Bishop of Winchester, William of Waynflete. It was in about 1470 that he began to restore the bridge, chapel and the Chapel House with the help of the cathedral mason John Cowper. A new phase began for St Mary's when a monastic inn was built and opened to welcome pilgrims, who would have entered the courtyard under the impressive archway. A fragment of this archway displaying the Plantagenet rose, the bishop's mitre and other religious symbols can be seen in the North Hall.

St Mary's had ceased to be a monastic building before the Dissolution of the Monasteries, having passed to Magdalen College, the beneficiary of Waynfete's estate. By the authority of Magdalen College the 'Chappil House and Seller' passed from John de Braose to his great-nephew, Sir Ralph Shirley, who had earlier inherited Wiston Manor. In turn, St Mary's was passed onto his grandson, Francis Shirley. By 1555 Shirley was a Member of Parliament for Shoreham and in 1574 was appointed Sheriff of Surrey and Sussex. He died in 1578.

As the chapel fell from use the name 'St Mary's' began to be applied to the house itself, which was now a much more grand, two-storey building. It was rumoured that Queen Elizabeth I was about to visit western Sussex on one of her 'progresses'. Since her Treasurer-at-War, Thomas Sherley [sic] lived at Wiston, the most likely place for her to stay would have been with him at the manor, but Queen Elizabeth disliked the man so it was only natural that she would have preferred the hospitality offered at St Mary's. Legend informs us that itinerant painter-stainers were hurriedly brought in to decorate the upper chamber with *trompe-l'oeil* panels depicting scenes of battle with galleons in full sail, believed to be the fleet of King Henry VIII in battle with the French in 1545. As no records exist we will never know for sure if the visit actually took place, but an interesting photograph of St Mary's was taken by a Brighton photographer, William Cornish, in 1860, and the caption reads: 'The house at Bramber at which Queen Elizabeth put up during her Summer Tour through the south of England'.

During the seventeenth century it has been suggested that the ancient building suffered considerable damage in what became known as the 'Bramber skirmish', when the Royalists tried to sieze the bridge. The whole of the western wing seems to have disappeared during this time, exposing the courtyard to the street, as well as the southern and eastern wings, but as no records exist it could equally have suffered a fire. There is also a story that Charles II stayed at Bramber on his way to France. Having taken the road from Boscobel to Lyme Regis, he became more frustrated as he tried in desperation to find a ship that would take him to France and he descended the Downs into Bramber. It is claimed that when the Parliamentary troops were coming into the village to find food, they jostled the royal party as they passed in the direction of St Mary's, where he reportedly spent the night before escaping through a secret door to catch a boat from Shoreham to Europe.

St Mary's passed out of the hands of the Shirley family to the Gough family, later the Gough-Calthorpes, and many changes were made to the house during their time there.

After almost 300 years in the hands of this family, the house was sold to Richard Hudson, a farmer and parish clerk of Bramber who bought the dilapidated building for £300. In 1896 it changed hands again when the Hon. Algernon Bourke and his wife Gwendolen bought and restored it, but a right-of-way to St Botolph's Church annoyed him so he sold the property to Albert Musgrave in 1899. He set about building a new road and bridge, moving the right-of-way, which pleased all concerned. Around this time Arthur Conan Doyle is said to have visited the house and used it as an influence to write his short story 'The Adventure of the Musgrave Ritual'.

The Edwardian period was a time of splendour at St Mary's, with many lavish parties for the high and mighty of the day taking place, but the First World War brought this era to an end. The years between the wars were again happy times at the house, which was now in the hands of the McConnel family, who often allowed the house to be used in their absence as a 'finishing school' for wealthy young American girls. There are romantic tales of young men flying over from Shoreham Airport and dropping love notes into the gardens for the young girls. It is said that the house was constantly filled with laughter, and one of the games that the McConnel children played with their young friends was called 'the King's Escape'. In the King's Room is a secret door, while a hiding place behind the chimney stack is reputed to have been used by Prince Charles prior to his escape to France.

In 1938 the family moved to the nearby village of Upper Beeding and the frivolities came to an end. At the outbreak of the Second World War, St Mary's was empty so was requisitioned by the Ministry of Defence and used as a billet for a number of regiments, including 150 Canadian troops in 1941. During this time the interior of the house suffered much damage due to vandalism as these young Canadians, fresh from the prairies, who didn't fully appreciate the medieval monastic inn they found themselves in.

By 1944 the house was threatened with demolition but was saved by a strange coincidence, one of several that have happened down the years. A Miss Dorothy Ellis went to her hairdressers in London and was given a magazine to read and noticed an advertisement for the sale of St Mary's. Against advice, Miss Ellis decided to attend the auction being held at the Ship Hotel in Brighton and soon found she was bidding against a builder who wanted to demolish St Mary's for its timber. Thankfully she won, but was dismayed to find the wartime blackouts were still in place, much of the wall-covering lay on the floor, the panels in the Painted Room were scratched and the beautiful 300-year-old leather was torn. Ivy was growing in the Music Room and on the walls in the hall, in 12-inch high lettering, were the words 'Home Sweet Home' in red paint. She set about furnishing twelve of the thirty rooms, with the intention of opening it up to visitors. Her achievements can never be underestimated, but by 1979, now advancing in years, she was forced to sell St Mary's. For three years the author and lepidopterist Paul Smart lived at St Mary's and continued to open it to the public, together with his extensive butterfly collection, but by 1983 the contents had to be sold and St Mary's remained empty for over a year.

In November 1984 the Thorogood and Linton families bravely joined forces and stepped in to save the house in its hour of need. Today the house is open to the public from May to September – see www.stmarysbramber.co.uk for details – and is well worth a visit.

The Warden's Room. When St Mary's was a monastic inn for pilgrims, this room provided accommodation for the wardens of the bridge at Bramber.

As for the ghostly encounters, there are several and from different periods of history. It is not surprising to hear that there are sighting of monks, and Peter Thorogood told me that when he moved in a monk used to continually knock. It is thought that an underground tunnel leads from the Church of St Bololph's in Upper Beeding and passes under the south garden, which may explain the knocking on the doorway. Obviously the monk is happy with its restoration, as Mr Thorogood reports he has been silent for a while. Mr Thorogood can often smell incense in the Hall, which is adjacent to the Warden's Room, where the four monks provided by Sele Priory would have had their cells. Today the room is used as a morning room and is where visitors are first introduced to the story of St Mary's. The Canadian soldiers billeted at the St Mary's during the Second World War reported a mysterious monk seen wandering about in Monk's Walk, and land girls were frightened when they reported seeing monks in the vicinity.

Several people have reported a musky perfume smell in the bedroom above the Painted Room, reportedly decorated for Queen Elizabeth I, and also outside the Painted Room itself. Roger Linton himself, and his mother and his father, the Revd Laurence Linton, have experienced the smell in these areas.

Who, one wonders, is the pretty little Elizabethan child, dressed smartly in doublet and hose with a black velvet hat with a feather, whom Mary, Peter's Thorogood's sister, saw playing happily on the upper landing and looking down the stairs with a cheeky smile on her face? Is she waiting excitedly for the arrival of Queen Elizabeth I? Did she belong to

The Painted Room, hurriedly created for a visit of Queen Elizabeth I.

The entrance hall where incense has been smelt.

Left: *Mimi McConnel with Alice Patterson in the 1930s. Mimi would send tapers up the chimney to attract the ghosts, and saw the ghost of a White Lady on the stairs.*

Right: *Shelagh McConnel in 1935, standing on the same spot where her grandmother saw the ghostly White Lady.*

the household of the time or is she is visitor? If only the walls could talk, what stories they would tell.

Another apparition that was seen by Sheelagh McConnel's grandmother, Mimi, around 1935 is that of a White Lady who appeared several times on the stairs. Mimi McConnel, who was very much into ghosts, would send lighted tapers up the large inglenook chimney in the monk's parlour in the hope of enticing the ghosts down. Who is the mysterious White Lady and what is her connection with St Mary's? Obviously these ghosts are part of the fabric of the building and are content in their surroundings. They must feel very proud that its owners have saved St Mary's for future generations to enjoy.

Storrington

Approximately ten miles north of Worthing sits the village of Storrington at the foot of the South Downs, in the heart of West Sussex. Storrington is mentioned in the Domesday Book as 'Estorchestone' meaning 'a place well known for storks'! Tanning, blacksmithing and rabbit breeding were the industries of the day, which may account for so many place names including the word 'warren' in their titles.

Who Muddied the Envelope?

At No. 3 High Street is the fascinating 400-year-old coaching inn, the White Horse. The building dates back to 1535 and may once has been called the Half Moon or the Anchor. Recently the hotel has been tastefully refurbished in a contemporary style without losing any of its character. From 1940 to 1952 the Irish composer and poet Sir Arnold Bax lived at the White Horse. It was perhaps not the ideal place for him live, with its well-stocked

The White Horse in Storrington.

bar, as he battled growing difficulties with depression and alcoholism. He died in Cork in 1953 and is buried in Ireland.

The White Horse is reputed to have a rather playful, mischievous ghost who is generally friendly and is thought to be the ghost of an ex-landlord, but it is not certain which one. Several landlords over the years have experienced the high-spirited nudger who enjoys giving its victim a sharp push or shove. Perhaps the ex-landlord is trying to say it is still his pub! This sort of incident is not unusual, but this cheeky ghost decided to go a step further when he picked up one ex-landlady, lifting her off her feet. As with most mild supernatural activity, there is a sharp fall in the temperature, footsteps and shuffling noises can be heard in the corridor, and a strange feeling of depression lingers in the room.

However, the most famous ghostly encounter concerns Sir Arnold Bax. Twenty-five years after he died, in 1977, a letter arrived addressed to his executors. As it was around Christmas time, the landlady put the letter in the composer's old room for safekeeping. After the festivities were over she went to collect it so that it could be returned to the Post Office and she found a large dirty mark on the envelope, which was fresh and, some say, looked as though the letter had been trodden on. Others say it looked like it had been dragged through the mud. This was most odd when you consider that the letter had been locked in the room the whole time!

5

Ancient Rings and Woods Linked by Ley-Lines

Cissbury Ring

About three miles north of Worthing sits Cissbury Ring, an important historical site for flint production during the Stone Age, dating back to between 3500 and 2500 BC. Over 150 mine shafts have been discovered, some as deep as 50ft, making it an extremely large tool-making factory. Evidence has shown that the tools, one of the most valuable commodities of the day, were exported as far afield as northern England and all over Europe. Most of the remains seen today belong to the Iron Age hill fort that was built around 250 BC as a symbol of power. It would originally have consisted of a massive rampart, with a deep ditch in front together with a timber fence to protect the stronghold. It is the second largest in size in England after Maiden Castle in Dorset. By about 50 BC the camp and its fortress had been abandoned but when the Romans arrived they saw its potential and most probably used it as an administrative and military station. However, around a century later the Saxons arrived and legend informs us that the early Saxon leader, Cissa, resided at Cissbury and between AD 1005 and 1020 the Saxon royal mint, which had been operating at Steyning, was transferred to Cissbury.

The site was used in Elizabethan times as a beacon and during the Second World War, for the Sussex Defence Scheme, trenches were dug and emplacements cut into the Iron Age ramparts. With so much history, there is little wonder that Cissbury Ring has a strange and eerie feel, especially at night. It is said that the Devil had a hand in building Cissbury Ring. It is alleged that when he was digging Devil's Dyke, a V-shaped valley on the South Downs he wanted to flood the area and destroy all the churches, the resultant clods of earth were thrown into a pile which became the Ring. However, the same story applies to Chanctonbury Ring too!

Ghosts of highwaymen are said to be plentiful in Sussex, but one, near Cissbury Ring, proved to be a hazard for traffic using the old coaching road from Lancing to Steyning. It is claimed that a highwayman worked along this trackway on the Findon boundary, targeting the long-distance coaches. Eventually he was captured, tried, convicted and sentenced to death; he was duly executed on the ancient coach road near where some of his crimes

Cissbury Ring, looking towards the Ring from Findon. (Anne Purkiss, 2007)

were committed, just below the Cissbury Ring. Before he was hanged he vowed 'to not sleep in his grave'.

A grave was dug and the corpse buried, but the next morning a passer-by discovered the body poking out of the ground, its face visible and the mouth wide open. Several attempts were made to bury the highwayman, but each time his body was later found on the top of the grave and, seemingly, he had no intention of ending his career. His spirit was seen mounted on a horse many times, and one story tells of a coach held up by a highwayman. The terrified occupants of the coach ordered the driver to run down the highwayman that was about to rob them. The coach driver cracked his whip and urged the horses to charge, but the horses and coach passed straight through the mounted man.

What became of the highwayman's body is unknown, but for many years agricultural workers and travellers passing this particular spot claim that at the last moment they would see a body in the middle of the road and, unable to stop, would 'bump' over a soft object lying lengthways across the road, then they would hear a 'clunk' as the wheels crushed the bones. They would rush back to the scene only to discover that no one was there. The ghostly figure of the highwayman and his spectral horse have not been seen below Cissbury Ring for many years, but perhaps one day he will be seen again.

Chanctonbury Ring

One of the most mysterious sites in the Worthing area must be Chanctonbury Ring ('Chanklebury' in Sussex dialect), situated to the north of Worthing off the A283 Washington road bordering the parishes of Washington and Wiston. Chanctonbury Ring is known for its Iron Age fort, dating to between the sixth and fifth centuries BC. It was also used by the Romans as a religious centre and two Roman temples were erected on the site; furthermore, some Bronze Age pottery has also been found on the site. This has led to many tales of ghosts, witchcraft and fairies. For the purpose of this book I will only concentrate on the ghostly encounters.

It is said that if you run around Chanctonbury Ring seven times on May Day, Midsummer's Eve or any other moonlit night, an apparition of the Devil will appear and

offer a bowl of milk (other versions say it is a bowl of soup or porridge). There is, however, one condition: you must walk around the Ring backwards, and if you accept the Devil's food he will take possession of your soul. If you only run around the ring three times the apparition of a lady on a white horse can also be seen.

The top of the site is crowned with beech trees, the tree of wishes in mythology and folklore. These were planted in 1760 by Charles Goring, a young man who lived to the ripe age of eighty-five at nearby Wiston House. After the trees were planted they were watered daily until the roots took a hold, but oddly the trees in the centre never grew very well and this could have been because they were planted on an old Roman temple. It is said that no birds sing from these trees because of the hauntings. Locals will inform you that it is impossible to count the trees, although some say there were 365 before the great storm of 1987 which destroyed most of them. Today there is a low wire fence around the trees and behind it are the trees which were replanted in the aftermath of the storm. They are at various stages of growth, and it will be many years before the trees reach the height of those that were not damaged or uprooted.

It is claimed that the old astrologer and druid, Prince Agasicles Synnesis, was a frequent visitor to the Ring during the early 1600s, and legend informs us that he died in the Ring after writing in charcoal, 'Bury me where I have fallen'.

Countless investigators and walkers to the site have heard and seen strange things, from the crying of a baby to chanting by monks. Some mediums have been attacked whilst at the Ring, which has led to finger marks being left on them. In August 1974 four men from the Ghost and Psychic Investigations Group decided to spend the night at Chanctonbuy Ring, and whilst walking to the centre of the Ring one of the men was lifted several feet off the ground and was suspended in mid-air for several seconds. During this time he cried out, 'No more, No more!' and was obviously in a great deal of pain. Finally he dropped to the floor and landed heavily on his back.

On other occasions strange voices have been captured on digital recorders and tapes which did not belong to anyone present at the time. People have also experienced sudden bouts of sickness and disorientation, and it is a place that many have difficulty staying after dark. Even horses shy away from the area. There have also been the sounds of thundering hooves of invisible galloping horses and the beat of drums, while the ghost of a man on a horse who gallops past without stopping has been seen. Some say this is Julius Caesar and the sounds are the horses of his army.

What is the Walking Druid Looking For?

One of the more frequent ghosts is that of a druid who walks with his head down low, apparently looking for something. Another ghost is said to be that of an old man who appears to be guarding something, although some believe the ghost is a Saxon killed during the Battle of Hastings. Whoever he was, or whether these two ghosts are one and the same, he seems to have disappeared after a hoard of Anglo-Saxon coins were ploughed up at Chancton Farm in 1866, just below the hill at Washington. Was this treasure what he was looking for?

In the 1930s Southern Railway ran excursions, with a supper and breakfast car, from Victoria Station in London as far as Steyning so that participants could take a moonlight walk to Chanctonbury Ring to witness the sunrise from the top, but a number of people were unable to stay the night on the Ring as they felt very uncomfortable. In 1930 Dr Phillip Goose of Steyning, who wrote *Go To the Country*, said, 'Even on bright summer days there is an uncanny sense of some unseen presence which seems to follow you about. If you enter the dark wood you are conscious of something behind you. When you stop IT stops; when you go on IT follows'.

In 1966, members of the Southern Paranormal Investigation Team decided to camp on the Ring, They arrived around 9.30 p.m. and set about lighting a fire while talking to a group of motorcyclists who were also camping there. Things were quiet until just after midnight, when they heard a strange crackling sound followed by the wailing voice of a woman coming from an apparition that was moving around outside the Ring. This was followed by a two-hour period of silence, until around 2 a.m. they heard the sound of a church organ and feelings of intense pain by those gathered on the Ring. By 2.30 a.m. the motorcyclists had left, saying that something really evil was happening. However, the paranormal group braved the night, still in pain, and when they left the Ring in the morning the pain eased and disappeared.

Clapham Wood

Lying four miles north-west of Worthing sits the modern village of Clapham, and it would seem that the village has moved at least three times. 'Clap' or 'Clop' means 'hill' and 'Ham' indicates

A flyer for excursions to Chanctonbury Ring.

an early Saxon settlement. A little rhyme attributed to an unknown Patching cleric would indicate that the village was originally sited on the hill where the church still stands:

> Hilltop't Clapham sitteth all replete
> Where God and De'il 'tis said doth meet.

It was normal for a village to move, particularly during the Black Death which raged throughout England during the fourteenth century. It has been suggested that the village may have moved from the hill to the Holt hamlet, and then, for some reason, to its present position. The Church of the Blessed Virgin Mary at Clapham is a small flint and stone building and it is believed a church has existed on the site since the eleventh century, when in 1073 William de Braose gave tithes from it to his college at Bramber. An interesting feature of the church is the fifteenth-century walled-up doorway on the north side. Legend informs us that the north side of a building has in the past has been associated with the source of supernatural energy. To prevent evil spirits from entering a church it became the practice for the north doors to be walled up, as with Clapham, although it is uncertain when this took place.

The north and western boundaries of Clapham Church are overshadowed by the dense Clapham Woods, which has been the location of numerous UFO sightings, paranormal activity and several unexplained murders that date back to 1970, as well as being associated with a satanic cult called the Friends of Hecate. However, for the purposes of this book I am going to report on the paranormal activity only. Interestingly, Clapham Woods, Chanctonbury Ring and Cissbury Ring are all reputed to be linked by a mystical triangle of ley lines and some believe that the lines and their crossing points vibrate a special psychic or mystical energy.

Almost all investigators of the woods agree that there is very something strange about them. Many people have complained of dizziness and cramp soon after entering and investigations of bushes and trees are continuing to see if there is a natural cause. However,

Clapham Church.

A blocked-up door on the north side of the church. Was this blocked to keep evil spirits away?

with such a strange atmosphere it is the ideal place to look for ghosts. There are many reports of a feeling of unease in certain parts of the wood and some of the strangest experiences have come at the place called the Crossroads, which is in fact south of Clapham between the A27 and the village itself. Some mediums have reportedly been hit by unseen forces which they feel want them to go away. This area was very overgrown, but with the introduction of the A27 and then the great storm of 1987 this area is less wooded than before and the atmosphere not so oppressive. However, people still experience the sensation of being watched or followed.

The other area of focus for ghosts is a location north of St Mary's Church, deep in the woods at a mighty tree known as the Altar Tree. It is a huge oak with knotted branches that spread out and dates back many hundreds of years. If only this tree could talk, I am sure that it could tell a tale or two. Some mediums have felt unwelcome here and whilst sitting on a log on the east side of the tree it feels like a presence comes up behind you quite fast and makes you get up and move away from this seat quickly. There is certainly a claustrophobic feel in this part of the woods, which is strangely lacking in sound; there are no birds singing, no rustling of trees and no wildlife inhabits the hedgerows. It has become a focus over the years for many pagans, who leave offerings at the tree for their gods and goddesses, and on the day I visited I found lottery numbers written on pieces of paper pushed into the tree. There were also remnants of ribbon tied to the tree which, judging by their state, had been there for many months.

Stuart Logan of COTC, whom I went to the woods with, told me that he has a good friend who, with three other witnesses, was on his way across the field at the back of the church towards the first part of the woods when he noticed something odd. Having negotiated the stile and been halfway across the field, the group turned back to see an old man in a cloth cap pushing his bike through the same field a few yards behind them. They noticed that it appeared to be an old-fashioned bicycle. When they climbed over the stile into the wood they looked back to see how the old man was going to get the cycle over it, but to their astonishment he and the bike had completely disappeared. A look around showed them that the man could not have got into any cover in that time. Was this a ghost from the past?

6

UFOs or Alien Spaceships?

Over the last forty years or so UFOs (Unidentified Flying Objects) have been reported throughout Britain, but according to the British UFO Research Association (BUFORA) there is around one sighting a week reported in Sussex. Local reports show that there have been a number of sightings in and around the Worthing area. In most cases they are nothing more than unidentified lights in the sky, although some have been identified as Chinese lanterns set off as pranks, whereas some would say that only a small percentage can be attributed to hoaxes. According to BUFORA, for every ten sightings that are explained, there is at least one which turns out to be inexplicable.

UFOs have been sited at Chanctonbury Ring around Midsummer Eve for several years, and in 1968 a group of people who decided to watch for UFOs reported feelings of intense cold and electrical shocks through the body, as well as difficulty breathing. On 1 November 1972, All Saints Day, a man was walking with a group of his friends in the Ring when they heard a strange noise from above. They looked up and saw a large object surrounded by a red glow, brushing the top of the trees. After the object moved off they noticed blue lights as well as what they can only describe as four windows on the top of the object. When the UFO reached the outskirts of the trees it hovered for a short time before it shot up into the sky and was lost from sight. In 1974, and again in 1979, similar sightings were reported, and in 1975 a bright orange object was seen over Cissbury Ring before it headed off in the direction of Chanctonbury, where it was seen by a woman walking her dog.

Recently there have been a number of sightings reported in the local papers. For example, four strange orange UFOs were spotted moving from the south-west over Shoreham and reported in the *Argus* on 14 March 2007. It appears that they were travelling at the same height, at the same speed and in the same direction, and were all much lower that a normal aircraft. The *Argus*, published on 10 October 2007, gave some recent Ministry of Defence (MoD) figures confirming that fifty-two sightings had been recorded over Sussex between 1998 and 2006, and that all the cases had been investigated by the Ministry as they could be attributed to unauthorised military or hostile action.

Another UFO was spotted rocketing across the Downs near Lancing by Michelle Huggert, which was reported by the *Argus* on 3 January 2008. It was described as being red and orange and not behaving like an aircraft because it made no noise and moved very fast before suddenly stopping. Yet another report appeared in the *Worthing Herald* on 31 July 2008 describing how Worthing residents had been left baffled when dozens of mysterious lights 'invaded' the seafront. Emails and telephone calls flooded into the *Herald* news desk from confused onlookers who watched as what appeared to be up to twenty-one orange ball-like lights moved across the night sky, all below cloud level, at around 10.30 p.m. on Saturday 25 July.

Worthing Cricket Club star Danny Barton said he watched in amazement from his home as the lights flew by, then he rushed down to the seafront with a camera, saying that he had never seen anything like it in all his life. They were unusually bright and extremely close to the house, which is why he was convinced that something weird was going on. He drove down to the beach and when he got just past the line of trees, one of the lights seemed to come along about 6ft off the ground, but as soon as he got nearer to the trees, it was like it was controlled. It lifted up over the trees and carried on upwards. Mr Barton then filmed some of the lights with his camera phone before discussing the phenomenon with some police officers who were passing and were equally confused.

Another resident, Marc Baldwin, filmed the lights from the front window of his lounge, and his footage clearly showed a number of the lights drifting across the Goring area, although he admitted he was staggered to catch on film the amazing sight of one light speeding across the sky, suddenly stopping and then moving slightly before finally darting away. 'No plane could do that. No helicopter could do that', he said. Mr Baldwin said he would like to see if there is any logical explanation, but he didn't have a clue what it was, but a few suggested explanations for the lights include Chinese lanterns, or slow-moving aircraft of some kind that were part of a light display from the Worthing Festival. David Crossley told the *Herald* that it was incredible. 'It's not a little green man I know that, I just don't know what it is', and he went on to say that he had got all of his marbles and didn't drink that much, but he knew he had seen something strange. Interestingly, UFO experts recorded numbers of people nationwide reporting sightings over that particular weekend, so perhaps something spooky was going on.

Other strange things have been spotted in the sky over Littlehampton too, prompting concern over extra-terrestrial activity. In a report in the *Midhurst and Petworth Observer* on 8 January 2009, a student saw a strange orange light on the previous Tuesday, and a man from Worthing saw two of the same objects on the Saturday. The student said he was driving along the seafront towards the East Beach cafe at around 5.45 p.m. when an orange light came up from the ground in the distance. At first he assumed it was a firework, but as he watched it rose from the ground in a vertical line and didn't explode.

Two months later, on the afternoon of 1 March 2009, mysterious wingless objects appeared to be travelling at high speed and were spotted in the sky over Shoreham. Mr Middleton told the *Bognor Regis Observer* on 2 March that initially it appeared to be a flock of birds flying over the South Downs, but when he took a closer look he realised it was about six to ten objects and they were anything but birds. He could not make out any form of a wing and then he noticed some disappeared, perhaps due to a cloud, before reappearing again. In a short space of time he said they could have been over the Worthing area.

Could all these eyewitnesses be mistaken, or is there something strange going on along the South Coast? Only time will tell us more, but it does appear that the area covered in this book has more than its fair share of sightings.

Select Bibliography

Books
Andrew Green, *Our Haunted Kingdom* (Mosby Wolfe, 1973)
Andrew Green, *Haunted Sussex Today* (S.B. Publications, 1997)
Arron Weedall, *Haunted Chichester and Beyond* (The History Press, 2008)
Chris Hare, *Worthing: A History* (Phillimore & Co. Ltd, 2008)
Colin Excell, *A Brief History of St Mary the Virgin, Sompting* (Self-published, 2006)
Frank Fox-Wilson, *The Story of Goring and Highdown* (Goring Book Association, 1987)
Jacqueline Simpson, *Folklore of Sussex* (The History Press, 2009)
Janet Cameron, *Paranormal Brighton and Hove* (Amberley Press, 2009)
Janet Pennington, *St Cuthman of Steyning: A Journey Through Time* (Steyning Museum and the
    Friends of St Andrews, 1993)
Judy Middleton, *Haunted Places of Sussex* (Countryside Books, 2005)
Judy Middleton, *Ghosts of Sussex* (Countryside Books, 1988)
Leslie Baker, *Old Angmering* (Angmering Parish Council, 1988)
Peter Underwood, *This Haunted Isle: The Ghost and Legends of Britain's Historic Buildings*
    (Harrap, 1984)
Rolf Zeegers, Lucy Ashby, Juliet Nye, *Littlehampton Revisited* (The History Press, 2007)

Newspapers and Magazines
Various issues of:

Worthing Herald
The *Argus*
Bognor Regis Observer,
Midhurst and Petworth Observer
Worthing Gazette and Herald
Littlehampton Gazette
Sussex County Magazine

Websites
Wikipedia (www.wikipedia.org)
Supernatural Tours (www.supernatural-tours.co.uk)
West Sussex Paranormal Investigations (www.wspi.co.uk)
Children of the City Paranormal Investigators (www.cotcpi.co.uk)
Angmering (www.angmeringvillage.co.uk)
West Sussex Past Pictures (www.westsussexpast.org.uk)
St Mary's, Bramber (www.stmarysbramber.co.uk)

My apologies for any sources I have inadvertently forgotten.